"At one time or another, all of us experience loneliness—not just solitude, but loneliness. In this unique and valuable study, Lydia Brownback draws from Scripture and experience to uncover the heart issues and responses that lead lonely Christians in healthy or unhealthy directions. Without downplaying the inescapable loneliness of living in a fallen world, *Finding God in My Loneliness* nonetheless finds abiding hope in the friendship of Jesus Christ."

Philip Graham Ryken, President, Wheaton College

Finding God in My Loneliness

Other Crossway Books by Lydia Brownback

Contentment: A Godly Woman's Adornment

Joy: A Godly Woman's Adornment

Purity: A Godly Woman's Adornment

Trust: A Godly Woman's Adornment

*A Woman's Wisdom: How the Book of Proverbs Speaks
to Everything*

Finding God in
My Loneliness

Lydia Brownback

WHEATON, ILLINOIS

Scripture quotations are from the ESV® Bible (The Holy Bible, English Standard Version®), copyright © 2001 by Crossway, a publishing ministry of Good News Publishers. Used by permission. All rights reserved.

All emphases in Scripture quotations have been added by the author.

Trade paperback ISBN: 978-1-4335-5393-6
ePub ISBN: 978-1-4335-5396-7
PDF ISBN: 978-1-4335-5394-3
Mobipocket ISBN: 978-1-4335-5395-0

Library of Congress Cataloging-in-Publication Data

Names: Brownback, Lydia, 1963- author.
Title: Finding God in my loneliness / Lydia Brownback.
Description: Wheaton, Illinois : Crossway, 2017. | Includes bibliographical references and index.
Identifiers: LCCN 2016031222 (print) | LCCN 2016034173 (ebook) | ISBN 9781433553936 (tp) | ISBN 9781433553943 (pdf) | ISBN 9781433553950 (mobi) | ISBN 9781433553967 (epub)
Subjects: LCSH: Christian women—Prayers and devotions. | Loneliness—Religious aspects—Christianity. | Loneliness—Biblical teaching—Meditations. | Encouragement—Religious aspects—Christianity. | Encouragement—Biblical teaching—Meditations.
Classification: LCC BV4844 .B764 2017 (print) | LCC BV4844 (ebook) | DDC 248.8/43—dc23
LC record available at https://lccn.loc.gov/2016031222

Crossway is a publishing ministry of Good News Publishers.

VP		27	26	25	24	23	22	21	20	19	18	17
15	14	13	12	11	10	9	8	7	6	5	4	3	2	1

With gratitude to God
for
the special women of the
Cazenovia Women's Bible Study,
who encouraged my soul on Thursday mornings.

And,

for
Elisabeth Elliot (1926–2015)

Contents

Part 3

LONELINESS REDEEMED

Truly, truly, I say to you,
unless a grain of wheat falls into the earth and dies,
it remains alone;
but if it dies, it bears much fruit.

John 12:24

Why Are We Lonely?

The unexpected snowfall brought the neighborhood together as we worked to clear cars and walkways before the early December sunset. "Looks like winter is here!" I called over to my friend next door.

"Indeed it is!" she replied. "And the timing of all this snow is perfect. After supper we're going to make hot chocolate and decorate the Christmas tree. The kids are really excited."

As I stood there picturing her happy family scene, I was suddenly buried under an avalanche of overwhelming loneliness. For the first time ever, I decided against getting a Christmas tree that year. The thought of having no one with whom to unwrap each memory-laden ornament from its tissue-paper hibernation was just too depressing. A casual conversation was all it took.

A few Christmases later, determined to have for myself the sort of holiday fun my neighbor enjoyed with her family, I invited a few girlfriends to my home for a tree-trimming party. One friend was especially enthusiastic, and I asked her, "Why is coming to my place so great when you've got your own tree to decorate and a husband and kids to do it with you?"

"Let me tell you how *that* goes," she replied. "We pick a day when we're going to do it, and I get treats prepared and Christmas music playing, and all the ornaments are set out on the table. And when I'm ready, everyone wanders in. But five minutes into it, phone calls and texts and whatever else distract them, so they grab a cookie and disappear. I wind up decorating the tree alone every year."

How eye-opening that was! Those pictures of others' lives that we get in our minds or see on social media are rarely the reality. Behind the smiles and accolades and images of family fun lie all the normal stuff of everyone's life: heartbreak, rejection, anxiety—and loneliness.

Single or married, young or old, man or woman—everyone experiences loneliness at various times and to varying degrees. No one is exempt. We were created for togetherness, which is why, even before the fall, God declared that man's aloneness was not good (Gen. 2:18). And immediately after his declaration, he created marriage. But marriage was never intended to be the ultimate, eternal remedy for loneliness. That's why the unmarried aren't doomed in this regard. God created human beings with a capacity for loneliness so that we would yearn for and find our all in him:

> In Genesis 2 God ordains the marriage of male and female as another aspect of his design for our aloneness. Yet he never designed marriage to fulfill the incompleteness or eradicate the aloneness. Rather, it more fully reveals our need for our ultimate destiny—to be in union with him.[1]

In other words, loneliness is an indicator that something is missing, and that something is found only in Jesus Christ. He completes what's missing, that thing we identify as "loneliness," beginning from the moment we are joined to him in faith and brought to completion in glory. In other words, the primary reason we are lonely is that we aren't home yet. God created us for communion with him, and therefore loneliness will be fully eradicated only when we get to heaven. That's why everyone— young or old, single or married—experiences loneliness. No one is exempt.

That being said, the loneliness we feel and the circumstances that make us aware of it arise because of man's fall into sin back in the garden of Eden. The loneliness we experience is a consequence of sin and has been ever since Adam and Eve disobeyed God. The couple hid from God after they ate from the forbidden tree, and that's also when they began to hide from each other. Loneliness began in the garden.

Let's make an important distinction right here at the beginning of this book: there is a difference between *loneliness* and *being alone*. Sometimes loneliness and aloneness overlap, and one can breed the other, but they are not the same thing. Some of the loneliest people live among many, while other people can exist day to day with limited human contact and feel no lack. Why is this? What makes the difference? Thinking through these things helps us cultivate a deeper understanding of ourselves, our family and friends, and our Lord.

Loneliness is everywhere, but we don't talk about it too often. Perhaps that's because we've grown so accustomed to its oppressive weight that we've lost awareness of it altogether. Oh, something seems off, but we attribute it to the weather or the stress *du jour*, and we try to shake it off with a good dinner or a night out on the town. But there it is again the next morning.

Relief comes only as we acknowledge our loneliness and turn

to God and his Word for the help and understanding we need. That's where this book aims to take us.

We will start out by asking—and then seek to answer—a basic question: *Why are we lonely?* And then we'll see that the best remedy for loneliness in this lifetime is found in something Jesus said: "Whoever finds his life will lose it, and whoever loses his life for my sake will find it" (Matt. 10:39).

We'll also look at how God works in and through loneliness in the lives of his people. From the patriarchs in Genesis up through the present day, we will see that loneliness isn't something to fear but something that God redeems. In Scripture we discover that God is present in our loneliness. He is there in times of grief and in times of discouragement. He is there when others forsake us, and when our hopes are disappointed. He never leaves us, not even when our loneliness springs from our sin and bad choices.

Ultimately, what we're going to see is that those who belong to God through Christ Jesus are never really alone, and because that's true, loneliness does not have to characterize us. Isn't that a relief? As you join me in exploring this challenging issue, I pray that we all would come to a fuller understanding of who God is for us in Christ our Lord.

Part 1

LONELINESS REINFORCED

Hence, all earthly treasure!
Jesus is my Pleasure,
Jesus is my Choice.
Hence, all empty glory!
Naught to me thy story
Told with tempting voice.
Pain or loss, or shame or cross,
Shall not from my Savior move me
Since He deigns to love me.

Evil world, I leave thee;
Thou canst not deceive me,
Thine appeal is vain.
Sin that once did blind me,
Get thee far behind me,
Come not forth again.
Past thy hour, O pride and power;
Sinful life, thy bonds I sever,
Leave thee now forever.

—Johann Franck, "Jesus, Priceless Treasure"

1

Treasuring the
Wrong Treasure

"I can't seem to make my life work," Lanie complained to her friend. "I've spent years trying, but I can't find what I'm looking for."

And it's true. Over the past decade Lanie has started her life over, three separate times in three different states—new job, new church, new friends, new home. Well-meaning loved ones tell her what's missing is a husband. All she needs, they say, is a man to love and settle down with. But Lanie has had opportunities for marriage, so in her case that just isn't it.

Lanie can't explain what exactly isn't working in her life, although a pattern is clear. After a few years in a particular place, she gets a sense that something is missing, and a restlessness sets in; so in an attempt to obtain that missing something, she starts everything over again. The pattern has become a cycle—a vicious cycle—because wherever she goes, inevitably there is something missing. Lanie doesn't connect that missing thing with loneliness, but it is there, and it adds to the viciousness of the cycle. Every time she uproots, she intensifies her loneliness.

So what is Lanie's chief problem, and what is her real need?

The Loneliness of Freedom

A major contributor to Lanie's loneliness is, surprisingly, freedom. Never before has it been easier for women to pick up and go. Women today are well equipped; we've got financial investments, cutting-edge modes of transportation, and sophisticated street smarts. But the reality is that so much freedom can actually increase our loneliness. Today, because we no longer have to stay in one place and do life with the people also staying in this place, we don't make commitments. After all, why commit if we don't have to? Why risk getting stuck in undesirable circumstances, perhaps missing the fulfillment that lies right around the next bend in the road? But this view of freedom—the one thrown at us from everywhere today—actually robs us of the very thing it promises. In earlier eras, when there was less freedom, people made commitments—to a marriage, a job, a place—because they had no other options. And if you do some digging, you'll likely discover across the societal board that loneliness was less pronounced then, when people committed just because their choices were so limited.

Today we can all too easily follow what Barry Cooper calls the "god of open options." He writes:

> The god of open options is a cruel and vindictive god. He will break your heart. He will not let anyone get too close. But at the same time, because he is so spiteful, he will not let anyone get too far away because that would mean they are no longer an option. On and on it continues, exhausting

and frustrating and confusing and endless, pulling towards and then pushing away, like the tide on a beach, never finally committing one way or the other. We have been like the starving man sitting in front of an all-you-can-eat buffet, dying simply because he would not choose between the chicken and the shrimp. The god of open options is also a liar. He promises you that by keeping your options open, you can have everything and everyone. But in the end, you get nothing and no one.[2]

Finding Our Life

This sort of thing has definitely contributed to Lanie's loneliness. But the root of it is even simpler than that. Take a closer look at Lanie's dominant refrain: "*I can't seem to make my life work.*" Who is she focused on? Who is she living for? It's all there to see: Lanie has been living for Lanie. But are we—you and I—really that much different? Chronic loneliness and a sense of ongoing restlessness can be tip-offs that we're more like Lanie than we've realized. We, along with Lanie, need to see that whenever our primary pursuit is self-fulfillment, we're sure to miss it. Conversely, if we pursue Christ above all, we'll find what we've been restless for all along. Self-seeking breeds loneliness; self-forgetfulness breeds fullness. It's what Jesus was getting at when he said, "Whoever does not take his cross and follow me is not worthy of me. Whoever finds his life will lose it, and whoever loses his life for my sake will find it" (Matt. 10:38–39).

Self-seeking leads to the loss of real life, and our experience of this loss is often what we define as "something missing." It's what sends us on a perpetual search for that one next thing. For many of us, that one next thing seems to lie in the relational arena. Single women want to be married. Married women want a better marriage. Childless women want babies. Mothers want happier children. Empty-nesters want grandchildren. For others, that one next thing is more about accomplishing something important or having more meaningful work. There's nothing wrong with these desires—we're hardwired to want them. But at the same time, if we live to get them, we're sure to find them hollow when we do.

Look again at Jesus's words: "Whoever loses his life for my sake will find it." He is telling disciples that following him is costly, but what we gain is far greater than what we lose.

Choosing Our Treasure

So we have a choice. We can do all we can to hang on to our dreams and hopes and personal goals for life, love, and success in this world, or we can let go of those things as our primary reason to get out of bed every morning. But we will never make this choice unless our hearts grasp what it is we are meant to find instead. This *finding* comes out more fully in Jesus's parables:

> The kingdom of heaven is like treasure hidden in a field, which a man found and covered up. Then in his joy he goes and sells all that he has and buys that field. Again, the kingdom of heaven is like a merchant in search of fine pearls, who, on finding one pearl of great value, went and sold all that he had and bought it. (Matt. 13:44–46)

Is that how we see the kingdom of heaven? Do we value it as our greatest treasure? Simply realizing that it *is* our greatest treasure indicates that we're on the way to finding true fullness of life.

Theologians rightly teach that the best way to get at the true meaning of Jesus's parables is to find the main point and not get lost in the details, but it's still beneficial to consider the details too. All of God's Word is inspired, not just the main point. So, with that in mind, let's look a bit more closely at Jesus's words.

First, notice that the treasure is *something that was hidden*. On another occasion, Jesus was praying, and he said, "I thank you, Father, Lord of heaven and earth, that you have hidden these things [kingdom things] from the wise and understanding and revealed them to little children" (Matt. 11:25). Jesus was talking about the heart attitude necessary to understand and know God and to realize that he is the greatest treasure we'll ever have. So treasuring the right treasure begins with humility. It is revealed only to the humble.

Second, *finding the treasure brought joy*. We find joy in getting what we treasure. On the other hand, we do not find joy if we don't treasure what we get.

Third, *the treasure was worth letting go of everything else*. The only way we are going to know Christ as our supreme treasure is if we diminish the value of competing treasure. Anything—even good things—must go if they hinder Christ's lordship in our lives and hearts. If we cherish and cling to competing treasures, our affection for God will grow sluggish and our loneliness will only increase.

Notice also that everything owned by the treasure finder was sold in order to purchase the treasure; in other words, his possessions weren't merely given away. A truth we can glean from this detail is that the things we give up to follow Christ aren't without value in their own right. Sometimes laying hold of kingdom treasure will prove costly, but coming to know Christ as our greatest treasure is worth the cost.

When loneliness covers us like a blanket, our instinct is to look for a way out. When we don't know Christ as our treasure, we seek escape in whatever we can see in front of us—certain habits or indulgences, places we go, and even certain relationships. Not only are such things more ready at hand, it seems, but also, at some level, we tend to blame God for our loneliness. We won't know him as our greatest treasure if our view of him is skewed, and the more we seek escape from our pain in worldly things, the more warped our view of God becomes. Instead of looking for a way out of loneliness, we need to look at Jesus. Only then will we discover that he is what we've been looking for all along. And only then will we really be willing to "sell" our earthly possessions and acquisitions for the sake of God and his kingdom.

Jesus said: "If anyone comes to me and does not hate his own father and mother and wife and children and brothers and sisters, yes, and even his own life, he cannot be my disciple. Whoever does not bear his own cross and come after me cannot be my disciple. For which of you, desiring to build a tower, does not first sit down and count the cost?" And he concludes all this by saying, "Any one of you who does not renounce all that he has cannot be my disciple" (Luke 14:26–28, 33). A great deal of loneliness comes from either a reluctance or an outright unwillingness to follow Jesus if doing so means letting go of the way we want our life to work out.

Loneliness Fortified

We cling to our life in a variety of ways, one of which is a devotion to *laying up treasures on earth*. Jesus said, "Do not lay up for yourselves treasures on earth, where moth and rust destroy and where thieves break in and steal, but lay up for yourselves treasures in heaven, where neither moth nor rust destroys and where thieves do not break in and steal. For where your treasure is, there your heart will be also" (Matt. 6:19–21). In other words, devoting ourselves to acquiring material treasures isn't a good use of our lives because earthly treasures never last. They fall apart, or get stolen, and they certainly don't fill up our emptiness.

Attempting *to juggle competing treasure* is another way we cling to life on our own terms. But competing treasures are never equal—one will always dominate the other. That's why Jesus says we just can't do it, and because this world and what it offers often feel more real—and certainly more immediate in terms of the payoff—the self-centered, worldly competition can all too easily win.

Finally, we will remain entrenched in loneliness if we *seek a Savior without a cross*. Jesus said, "If anyone comes to me and does not hate his own father and mother and wife and children and brothers and sisters, yes, and even his own life, he cannot be my disciple. Whoever does not bear his own cross and come after me cannot be my disciple" (Luke 14:26–27). There is no discipleship without the cross, and in taking it up, we find the fullness of life that Christ promised.

We nod in agreement about the value of God's kingdom until it hits our personal brick wall. Do we have a nonnegotiable—something we aren't willing to part with in order to follow Christ? If so, it's no wonder we are lonely. Think about David Powlison's wise words:

> Fear and desire are two sides of a single coin. A sinful fear is a craving for something not to happen. If I want money, I fear poverty with its deprivations and humiliations. If I long to be loved, I'm terrified of rejection. If I fear pain or hardship, I crave comfort or pleasure. If I crave preeminence, I fear being subordinate to others.[3]

Loneliness Lifted

Getting at what we fear and desire or what makes us anxious is a good way to uncover what vies with Christ for top place in our hearts. If we are willing, we will come to see that we have nothing to fear in letting go of our self-oriented lives in order to follow Jesus. Just consider what he promised:

> Truly, I say to you, there is no one who has left house or brothers or sisters or mother or father or children or lands, for my sake and for the gospel, who will not receive a hundredfold now in this time, houses and brothers and sisters and mothers and children and lands, with persecutions, and in the age to come eternal life. (Mark 10:29–30)

We are quick to think, "Oh, yes, I'll have treasure in heaven, but right now, I'm here, and this is what I've got to deal with." But Jesus makes clear that enjoying Christ as our true treasure isn't just for heaven; it's for now too. The path out of loneliness begins by letting go of all our attempts to make life work on our own terms. It's about taking up our cross and following Jesus.

If loneliness is weighing us down, and if we find ourselves doubting that God really is our greatest treasure, we can be honest with him, our kind Father and friend. We can tell him that we've been trying so hard to make our life work the way we want that we've lost sight of all he is for us in Christ. We can ask him to show us afresh who he really is and to change our heart. Sometimes change begins with praying, "God, I'm willing to be willing." If that's the best we can do today, God will meet us there. He is more eager than we are that we come to treasure him above all else, and it is only as we seek him that we'll find what we have been looking for all along.

• • •

Questions for Discussion or Reflection from Chapter 1

1. How do today's many freedoms contribute to loneliness? How has this played out in your own life?

2. Discuss or describe what Barry Cooper calls "the god of open options."

3. How do Jesus's words in Matthew 10:38–39 speak to the issue of loneliness?

4. From the parables of the hidden treasure and the pearl of great price (Matt. 13:44–46), list the steps involved in laying hold of Jesus as our greatest treasure.

5. In Luke 14:26–33, Jesus explains the nature of true discipleship. Are you allowing something or someone to hold you back from following Jesus fully? If so, can you identify how your reluctance to let it go contributes to your loneliness?

"Let not your heart be troubled," His tender word I hear,
And resting on His goodness, I lose my doubts and fears;
Though by the path He leadeth, but one step I may see;
His eye is on the sparrow, and I know He watches me. . . .

Whenever I am tempted, whenever clouds arise,
When songs give place to sighing, when hope within
     me dies,
I draw the closer to Him, from care He sets me free . . .
His eye is on the sparrow, and I know He watches me.

—Civilla Martin, "His Eye Is on the Sparrow"

2

The Lies of Loneliness

Giving way to panic has proven helpful in a crisis—said no one ever. Yet panic is the natural response of those who fixate on their circumstances rather than on Christ. Didn't Peter prove this when walking on water? So long as he kept his eyes on Jesus, he made forward progress, but the minute he turned his gaze to the wind and the waves, he began to sink. Peter panicked (Matt. 14:22–30).

We often do the same thing when the wind and the waves of loneliness threaten to sink us. If we aren't fixed on Jesus—and if we don't view life through a biblical lens—we're going to try to fight those waves ourselves, and eventually we will go down. Panicked swimmers often drown.

Lie: Loneliness Is Pure Evil

Heightening the waves of loneliness is this myth: "Loneliness is a result of something bad, and therefore no one should have to experience it."[4] If we believe that, we're going to use everything we've got to fight against it. We will have no peace, no joy, and no delight in the Lord. And we will never find our way out of the water.

Let's take a closer look at that myth. Is loneliness really the result of something bad? On one hand, God did say that it's not good for man to be alone (Gen. 2:18). So in that sense, yes, aloneness—and its accompanying loneliness—is not good. Yet we can't escape the fact that it was God himself who made Adam and then put him in the garden all alone. Sin hadn't even entered the world yet. In other words, Adam's aloneness was God's doing, and God did it so that Adam—and all human beings after him—would yearn for companionship. God went on to provide a wife for Adam; however, "he never designed marriage to fulfill the incompleteness or eradicate the aloneness. Rather, it more fully reveals our need for our ultimate destiny—to be in union with him."[5] So from the beginning man's aloneness wasn't good per se, but that wasn't the end of the story. No, God went on to provide the remedy for it. So there's no need to panic. The emptiness that so often accompanies aloneness—loneliness—is meant to be filled to the full with Christ.

Lie: I Shouldn't Have to Be Alone

So aloneness isn't all bad after all. And since that's the case, we can't really claim that no one should have to experience it. To the contrary, since God designed us to yearn for connectedness, it stands to reason that we *must* experience loneliness. Apart from that, we'd be prone in our natural selfishness to isolate ourselves so we can have everything in life our own way, never having to bend to the wishes and needs of others. Without a biblical perspective, we will see loneliness as utterly bad, as something to avoid at all costs. And we will panic.

The voice of panic says,

I'm the only one who's home alone tonight.

He's less than ideal, but if I don't marry him, I might never have another chance.

Being alone is going to ruin my health.

If God were truly good, he wouldn't leave me in this lonely situation.

God says,

Be strong and courageous. Do not be frightened, and do not be dismayed, for the LORD your God is with you wherever you go. (Josh. 1:9)

I will never leave you nor forsake you. (Heb. 13:5)

And Jesus said,

Behold, I am with you always, to the end of the age. (Matt. 28:20)

What happens when we panic? Our heart races; we can feel the blood pound. A sense of desperation rises up in our throat—we can almost taste it. And then our mind scrambles to latch on to a way out, and at this point, any way will do. If you're like me, those moments occur most frequently after sundown. Sometimes I dread the night. How will I make it through another one all alone? And *why must I*? That's what it comes down to, isn't it? Panic so easily morphs into rebellion. Once that happens, we've turned away from God rather than toward him. We reject God's comfort and turn to whatever escape is nearby—television, Facebook, food, alcohol, sleep. We don't want comfort on God's terms, so we say, "Thanks, but no thanks." Yet if we insist on life on our terms, we will only entrench our loneliness.

Lie: I Can Fix This Myself

Sometimes our escape methods are significantly more sophisticated. We don't settle for that simple evening escape; we strat-
egize a radical life-turnaround. And indeed there are times when
undertaking a significant change might be a wise approach.
God's blessings often come to us by means of our own activity,
and a pressing weight of loneliness might be the very thing God
is using to redirect our path. But if the only available options
for change are biblically questionable or if godly friends express
reservations about our plans, then we are wise to reconsider.
And even when it's all systems go, there is no guarantee that
our loneliness will be remedied as a result. The bottom line is,
we can't fix our loneliness; we haven't been created with that
capability. We can alter our aloneness, but not our loneliness.

The Light of Truth

So what's our goal? That's a good question to ask ourselves
if loneliness is compelling us to consider a major life change.
If we are believing the lies—aloneness is bad, I shouldn't have
to be lonely, and I can fix my loneliness—then those lies are
going to drive us. That relocation we're considering might
open all kinds of new doors, but it won't necessarily solve
loneliness. Signing on with Match.com might result in a relationship, but there's no guarantee it will remedy loneliness. The
church across town has a lot more people, but leaving a small
church for a larger one can backfire as a loneliness remedy. On
the other hand, if we're lonely because we have no Christian
fellowship or Bible-believing church to attend, then making a
change is a wise plan.

So goal assessment, done prayerfully through time in God's
Word, is a good way to begin when it comes to quelling panic.

For those of us who are lonely because we are alone, here's something else we can ask ourselves: Is my aloneness *really* so bad? If we believe the lie that being alone is inherently bad, than we've got our answer. But as we think about the fact that, by God's design, aloneness has a good purpose, we might answer differently. After all, it was Jesus himself who sought to be alone at times just to commune with his Father (Matt. 14:23; Mark 1:35; Luke 6:12).

If our perspective on those alone times changes, we might be pleasantly surprised to discover that we actually prefer some evenings all to ourselves. How freeing to recognize that turning off the television and letting in the silence isn't the approach of death.

Conversely, we might discover that a God-given way out of our aloneness has been right in front of us all along, but we were unwilling to see it. Paul shows us one of those ways:

> For by the grace given to me I say to everyone among you not to think of himself more highly than he ought to think. . . . For as in one body we have many members, and the members do not all have the same function, so we, though many, are one body in Christ, and individually members one of another. Having gifts that differ according to the grace given to us, *let us use them.* (Rom. 12:3–6)

And so does John:

> That which we have seen and heard we proclaim also to you, so that you too may have fellowship with us; and indeed our fellowship is with the Father and with his Son Jesus Christ. . . . God is light, and in him is no darkness at all. If we say we have fellowship with him while we walk in darkness, we lie and do not practice the truth. *But if we walk in*

the light, as he is in the light, we have fellowship with one another. (1 John 1:3, 5–7)

Married or single, young or old, rich or poor—we cannot fix our loneliness. But we can put it to use. The real question is, are we willing? Willingness is possible only by replacing the lies we've believed with the truth. Elisabeth Elliot writes:

> When the surrender of ourselves seems too much to ask, it is first of all because our thoughts of God Himself are paltry. . . . In our blindness we approach Him with suspicious reserve. We ask how much of our fun He intends to spoil, how much He will demand from us, how high is the price we must pay before He is placated. If we had the least notion of His lovingkindness and tender mercy, His fatherly care for His poor children, His generosity, His beautiful plans for us; if we knew how patiently He waits for our turning to Him, how gently He means to lead us to green pastures and still waters, how carefully He is preparing a place for us, how ceaselessly He is ordering and ordaining and engineering His Master Plan for our good—if we had any inkling of all this, could we be reluctant to let go of . . . whatever we clutch so fiercely in our sweaty little hands?[6]

Lies about loneliness are dislodged only by truth about God. He has not left us to solve our plight on our own. Nothing has slipped through the cracks. We are not stuck in Plan B, no matter what brought us to the place we're in today. If we are alone—if we are lonely—the ache of it is God calling us to deeper fellowship with him through his Son.

Peter began sinking in the wind and the waves because he took his eyes off Jesus. Once that happened, he could see no way out, no rescue. But rather than fight harder to save himself, he cried out, "Lord, save me." And immediately—with no delay, no conditions—Jesus reached out and pulled Peter into the boat. Then he asked Peter a question: "O you of little faith, why did you doubt?" (Matt. 14:30–31).

• • •

Questions for Discussion or Reflection from Chapter 2

1. Read Matthew 14:22–31. What does Jesus say to Peter after pulling him from the waves? What had Peter done to warrant Jesus's rebuke?

2. Do your beliefs about loneliness determine your view of God, or do your beliefs about God determine your view of loneliness? Either way, how do your beliefs show up in the ways you deal with lonely seasons?

3. Describe a time when loneliness made you panic. What did you do? What was the outcome of how you handled it?

4. Why can't we fix our loneliness?

5. How do we know when loneliness might indicate a need for practical change?

Part 2

LONELINESS
REALIZED

I am a poor wayfaring stranger,
While traveling through this world of woe.
Yet there's no sickness, toil nor danger,
In that bright world to which I go.
I'm going there to see my Father,
I'm going there no more to roam;

I'm just a going over Jordan,
I'm just a going over home.

—Folk spiritual, "Wayfaring Stranger"

3

The Loneliness of Leaving

"There's no place like home," chants Dorothy as she clicks together the heels of the ruby slippers. No one who's ever been homesick can forget this stirring scene in *The Wizard of Oz*. It conveys so well the palpable yearning to get back to a place—*our* place—that we can't quite reach, for whatever reason. The rhythm of life in the place that shaped us—how could we ever have taken it for granted? We'd give anything to get back there. Often, home is understood as *home* only after we've left it.

Home is more powerful than we often realize. Its hold on our heart goes beyond the house we lived in with our parents, siblings, and pets. Home includes one's neighborhood and town, the nearest city, and outward from there to the state and the region of the country. Home is a culture. It includes climate and the activities that accompany that climate. It includes temperaments, habits, behaviors, and tastes in clothing, food, and home décor.

In ways big and small, home shapes us, and therein lies its power. Without our even realizing it, we are defined by home, but often we discover that reality only when we've gone to live somewhere else. And the discovery can be devastating. Until we experience it, we are surprised to find that a relocation is often placed third on lists of most painful experiences, just after the death of a child and a divorce. Until we've gone through a relocation, we imagine the hardest part of it is learning our way around a new place—nothing a GPS can't solve. But that's the easy part. The hard part is the identity crisis that begins to overtake us about six weeks in. It's not that everything is new and different. It's that the identity that home provided us no longer fits. *We don't know who we are anymore.*

Called Out

It is into this very experience of loneliness that God called Abraham. Along with his two brothers, Abraham had grown up in Ur, a thriving city by the standards of that day. Abraham was surely shaped by this cosmopolitan environment. When he was seventy-five years old, one of his brothers died, and his father uprooted the family, and they headed toward the land of Canaan. Among those who left Ur were Abraham and his wife, Sarah; his remaining brother; and his nephew Lot. The family never made it to Canaan, however; they settled instead in the land of Haran, an important center of commerce in the ancient world (Gen. 11:31–32). It was here in Haran that Abraham was called by God:

> Now the Lord said to Abram, "Go from your country and your kindred and your father's house to the land that I will show you. And I will make of you a great nation, and I will bless you and make your name great, so that you will be a blessing. I will bless those who bless you, and him who dishonors you I will curse, and in you all the families of the earth shall be blessed." (Gen. 12:1–3)

Implicit in the call is the very thing we've been talking about. Abraham was to leave everything he had ever known, all that had up until then shaped his life. He was being called away not only from familiar places and close relationships but also from how those people and places had defined him. In a nutshell, he was being called away from his old identity to go forward into a new one.

When we're young, such calls seem exciting, and we head out with anticipation into an unknown future. Yet so many of us return to the place of our roots a few years later, when we get serious about settling down. Abraham wasn't young. If you recall, he was seventy-five years old when the call came. But he heeded the Lord's directive: "Abram went, as the LORD had told him" (v. 4).

Although Abraham departed with his wife, his nephew, his servants, and his possessions, he knew he was breaking with his old identity, which is clear from how God worded the call: "Go from your country and your kindred, and your father's house." Yet he went without hesitation, and that's because God had also made clear that the *new* he was going toward would be better than the *old* he left behind. It was bound to be better because the call involved God's big-picture purposes. In other words, God's call of Abraham wasn't just about Abraham. The same is true for all who follow the Lord's call, wherever that call takes us. When following God leads us to part from the old and familiar for the new and unknown, we can be sure that God's plan for our individual life is somehow intertwined with his plan for the collective life of all his people. That new identity Abraham found is the same as ours—we are part of a people, the family of faith.

Between the Old and the New

Breaking with the old before realizing the blessing of the new—
that's commonly how God's calls come. And the path in between
old and new is where we know some of our deepest loneliness.
It's a pattern many experience, not just when they first come to
Christ but repeatedly thereafter. At times following God means
painful partings, yet what he leads us to always proves enrich-
ing, even though, while walking the road from the old to the
new, there are bound to be times of isolation and loneliness.

I don't know about you, but that's been my story and that
of many others. Why this pattern? It surely must be because
we cling to God most tightly and get to know him most deeply
when our earthly foundations are stripped away. The comfort
and familiarity of the old is behind us, and the fulfillment of
God's promises awaits a future day. What do we do in the meantime? Where do we turn to get some grounding under our feet?
This is when we realize our foundation is ultimately only in
the Lord.

In Abraham's case, he journeyed away from urban envi-
ronments to those that were sparsely populated, pitching his
tents in a strange land among strange people, the Canaanites.
But in the midst of his journey, God spoke to Abraham again
and reaffirmed his promise: "To your offspring I will give this
land" (v. 7). As he did with Abraham, our compassionate God
meets us while we are walking that lonely road and reaffirms
his promises. And it's there that we find that the loneliness isn't
some arbitrary consequence of the journey—in God's economy
loneliness is a primary aspect of it. In that lonely pit we are
made sufficiently vulnerable to hear God and embrace his ways
most fully. We see this divinely intended outcome in Abraham's
response: "So he built there an altar to the LORD, who had ap-

peared to him" (v. 7). And as Abraham journeyed on, we're told that he built another altar and that he "called upon the name of the LORD" (v. 8).

That being said, the fact of God's presence and promises doesn't negate the struggle as we walk a new path. Abraham eventually reached Egypt, another unfamiliar place with strange people and customs, and in the strangeness of it all, he reacted in fear rather than faith and relied on dishonest manipulation rather than the Lord's promise of protection. Even then, the Lord didn't leave Abraham to get himself out of trouble; he came to the rescue (vv. 10–20). Likewise, our response to the call of God is rarely a straight, easy line from here to there. So far as our faithfulness goes, it is so often two steps forward and one back; but despite that, God never wavers in his intentions to get us where we are going. He is faithful even when we are not (2 Tim. 2:13). So when loneliness closes in, when the waves of homesickness threaten to drown us, this is our comfort. And we begin to discover through God's presence and power that our identity is not bound up with where we've come from or where we are going next. It's found in God himself. He—not a place or a people—gives us our self-definition.

The Promise Ahead

Finding our identity in God is vital, which is why his call often entails a break from old ways and familiar paths. The break away is orchestrated by God himself, tailored in love to the individual he is calling. And then, when the way is painful—at times it surely will be—we remember the promises.

That's what Abraham did. God had promised to make him into a great nation and through him to bless all the families of the earth. And he held out to him a place for this nation to get established—the land of Canaan, the Promised Land. But this was no mere trade-off, leaving one life, one family, one set of friends, one place, and one routine for another. (There's no real blessing in leaving the old if the new we move toward is just more of the same.) The promise was ultimately about having everything—family, friends, place, and life itself—with God in his kingdom. Through Abraham would come the royal line, culminating in the King of kings, Jesus Christ himself. From Abraham's physical family would come the spiritual family of God's people, united to God and to one another through union with Christ, Abraham's ultimate descendant. The hope of something beyond this life—even the best things and relationships and places—is what Abraham discovered in and through his loneliness. And as he journeyed on the way God led him, his identity became to him less and less about either the old life back in Ur or the new life before him in Canaan and more about life in God's kingdom. We know that's true because he is included among those of whom the writer of Hebrews says:

> These all died in faith . . . having acknowledged that they were strangers and exiles on the earth. For people who speak thus make it clear that they are seeking a homeland. If they had been thinking of that land from which they had gone out, they would have had opportunity to return. But as it is, they desire a better country, that is, a heavenly one. Therefore God is not ashamed to be called their God, for he has prepared for them a city. (Heb. 11:13–16)

Is that our mind-set? It can be. And sometimes loneliness is the tool God uses to get us there. The leaving and the loneliness that accompany it are how he calls us out of our identity in this life to know the joy of being fully identified with him. That's what we see in Psalm 45, which was sung at the wedding of a king. The bride is told:

> Hear, O daughter, and consider, and incline your ear:
>> forget your people and your father's house,
>> and the king will desire your beauty.
> Since he is your lord, bow to him. (Ps. 45:10–11)

Ultimately, this psalm points to Jesus, the King of kings and the husband of his people. Do you see the call?

Choosing Our Path

Following Jesus means a shift in priorities. He becomes first so that when it comes down to either-or rather than both-and, we choose Jesus. And making that choice beautifies us in God's eyes.

The call to follow Jesus is radical, and it might very well lead us down lonely paths. A particular scribe who wanted to follow Jesus was warned that doing so might mean forgoing a comfortable home life (Matt. 8:20). Another man wanted to follow but not until his father had died. Jesus made him choose: "Follow me, and leave the dead to bury their own dead" (v. 22). That's the real question, isn't it? Are we willing to follow his call even if it means loss and the loneliness that springs from it?

If we don't consider all this beforehand, we are likely to turn back when the going gets rough. That's why Jesus warned would-be followers to count the cost before starting out (Luke 14:25–33). Following might cost us our career plans, our relationships, or the comforts of a mainstream middle-class life. It will most surely cost us our right to hang on to our old identity. That's the cost we have to count, because when that old identity falls away, we are likely to crash down if we aren't prepared for the significance of the loss and how bewildering the way forward can seem at times.

Although Abraham had been told on more than one occasion the great blessings he'd receive for following God, going forward required the obedience of faith: "By faith Abraham obeyed when he was called to go out to a place that he was to receive as an inheritance. And he went out, not knowing where he was going" (Heb. 11:8). We too have God's promises, but, like Abraham, we don't always know where following the Lord is going to take us. Will we trust him? Are we willing to set out, believing that where he is leading us will prove to be better than what we've left—even when we can't possibly see how? It's the only way to get through the loneliness of an identity crisis, of losing everything that up until now has defined who we are.

When we are feeling our way alone in the dark, we remember the promises. What we gain by following Christ is so much richer and longer lasting than anything we lose. At one point Peter said to Jesus, "We have left our homes and followed you" (Luke 18:28), and Jesus replied: "Truly, I say to you, there is no one who has left house or wife or brothers or parents or children, for the sake of the kingdom of God, who will not receive many times more in this time, and in the age to come eternal life" (vv. 29–30). That "many times more" has to do with home and family, the very things that so naturally define us in this life. Through the loneliness that comes from heeding this call, the Lord redefines us and gives us a whole new identity. As we follow, clinging to him as we go forward, we find that our real home and family are with him in the fellowship of his people. This isn't some nice-sounding spiritual concept—it's the real thing. Our affections are changed—part of our new identity—to make our spiritual home a reality in our hearts and lives. And this isn't just for later, in heaven. Jesus says it's also "in this time."

Is your loneliness due to an identity crisis? If so, you won't regain that old identity by going back home. Those who try usually find that it just doesn't work. You won't find it in the new place either. That's because God doesn't want you to. He wants you to know that you're already home. In Christ, you have your true identity, "for those whom he foreknew he also predestined to be conformed to the image of his Son, in order that he might be the firstborn among many brothers. And those whom he predestined he also called, and those whom he called he also justified, and those whom he justified he also glorified" (Rom. 8:29–30).

• • •

Questions for Discussion or Reflection from Chapter 3

1. As you reflect on your life to date, how has home shaped you? How does home play into your self-identity?

2. Why does God call Abraham to leave his home? How did the call of Abraham go beyond just Abraham himself to God's big-picture purposes? Review Genesis 12:1–7 and Hebrews 11:13–16.

3. Have you left home to pursue a particular calling—a job or a marriage, perhaps? If so, how did the change impact you? What have you learned about God in the transition?

4. How does God work in us through a call away from old familiar ways to produce spiritual growth?

5. What truths about God can strengthen our hearts when we are going through an identity crisis? Can you think of additional Scripture passages besides those mentioned in chapter 3?

When darkness shrouds your lonely path,
And long and dreary seems the way,
With aching heart and tearful eyes
You sigh in vain for break of day,
O pilgrim, then look up; behold!
A Bright light shining in the sky,
The "Bright and Morning Star" appears;
He'll wipe the tears from ev'ry eye.

He comes to bind the broken heart;
He comes to make the darkness light,
To guide your weary feet to find
The blessed morn that hath no night.
And when your soul shall joyful rise
To its celestial home on high
The Lord shall lead you tenderly,
He'll wipe the tears from ev'ry eye.

—Amelia Minerva Starkweather,
"When Darkness Shrouds Your Lonely Path"

4

The Loneliness of Night

Are you a morning person or a night owl? Morning people awaken early, eager to dive into the day, and are typically most productive in the hours before noon. That's me to a tee. Rain or sun, summer or winter, at home or in a hotel—I love morning. There's always this quiet expectation of yet untapped potential, unmarred by anxiety and the cares of life that inevitably creep in by lunchtime. As the cares mount up, creativity drains away in the fight against stress. By dinnertime, we morning people are glad the day is over, and we often prefer to do nothing but unwind until bedtime. I've never understood night owls, those who don't feel fully alive until the sun is far up in the sky and whose energy only increases as the day progresses. These are the ones who can settle in happily at the computer at 8:00 p.m. for a four-hour writing session or head out to a party when the rest of us are preparing for bed.

The Dread of Night

I dislike night. I've always disliked it, from the time I was a little girl. In fact, as a child I dreaded night. I was terrified of sleepovers at the home of friends. What if I awoke in the middle of the night? Who could I turn to for comfort in the dark? Not my sleeping friends and certainly not their parents! The fear of waking up alone was so intense that I'd lie awake until my tears resulted in my mother being called to come take me home.

Can you relate? Have you ever dreaded night? If so, it's likely that the dread has diminished with age but perhaps not the dislike. In fact, for many of us the dislike spreads out, backing up from night to earlier in the evening, and every day we brace ourselves as the sun begins to set. Can we perhaps make a connection between our dislike of the dark and loneliness? Surely it is lurking in there somewhere.

Many single women dread coming home from work at the end of the day, with four long hours to get through before bedtime. We reach a certain age where going out every night just isn't physically feasible or wise, so we must come up with some way to fill those hours—something low-key because we are too worn out from the day to do anything that requires much energy.

Solitary women aren't the only ones who dread night. It's also a difficult time of day for those experiencing a season of marital disharmony. Wife and husband sit silently through the evening meal and afterward drift into separate rooms to avoid the obligation to communicate. But bedtime is the worst. The loneliest women I know aren't single women—they are those in a difficult marriage. There's nothing lonelier than lying awake next to someone you can't seem to talk to.

Nighttime is also fear-filled for mothers of wayward and rebellious teens. Are their children out with a bad crowd, perhaps drinking and driving or taking other kinds of risks? Their heart jumps into their throat every time the phone rings. While such maternal fears can occur at any time of day, they are more pronounced at night, because people—teens *and* adults—can more easily do in the dark what they don't want seen in the light. As the apostle Paul noted, "Those who sleep, sleep at night, and those who get drunk, are drunk at night" (1 Thess. 5:7).

So for a variety of reasons, whether single or married, nighttime for many is a daily chore to simply get through. The question is, what can we do about it? Is there a cure for the dread of long evening hours? Many of us seek a remedy by observing what others do. And we ask our friends how they spend their evenings in hopes of learning something we've somehow missed. Here's some of what we're told:

> Downtime—are you kidding me? By the time dinner is cleaned up and the kids are in bed, I'm too tired to do anything but jump in bed and read for a few minutes until I drift off.

> After the dishes are done, Ben and I will take a walk, but if it's raining, we'll play a game or pick out a movie to watch.

> I make a few phone calls, and then I catch up on emails and maybe pay some bills.

> Evenings at home? I can't even tell you the last time I was home much before bedtime. I have church activities two or three nights a week, and the other nights I go to the gym and then meet a friend for dinner.

It all sounds so simple, but somehow, for whatever reason, those activities don't work for us the way they work for others. I am baffled by—and not a little bit envious of—those who can slip so easily from day into night. Why can't I find a routine that works for me—some rhythm of life in which joy, peace, and a sense of well-being don't depend on daylight? Some of us are stuck at this very point.

Stuck in the Dark

Nighttime "stuckness" doesn't happen overnight. Chances are, the reason we are stuck today is that somewhere along the way, earlier on, we made a choice to cope with evening loneliness by simply escaping the problem altogether. Rather than turn to the Lord for help, we turned to television. Or perhaps we did turn to the Lord, but our cries for help seemed unanswered so in frustration or discouragement we turned to food or alcohol or sleeping pills or to a relationship that falls outside of biblical bounds. And now, after weeks or months or even years of indulging our particular form of escape, we can't imagine for ourselves anything different. If that's where we find ourselves today, no doubt we are miserable. That's because, rather than escape the darkness, we have actually entrenched ourselves in it.

But those in Christ don't belong there, because God "has delivered us from the domain of darkness and transferred us to the kingdom of his beloved Son" (Col. 1:13). Once our spiritual darkness ends, nighttime darkness loses its former power too. The dark of night has no more say over us. We have a choice. When it comes to our well-being, night can be the same as day. Look at what Jesus said: "I am the light of the world. Whoever follows me will not walk in darkness, but will have the light of life" (John 8:12). Day or night, Jesus is our light. So we have nothing to fear when the sun goes down.

If we count ourselves among those united to Christ yet we continue to escape reality by numbing ourselves at the end of each day, how did we end up in this place? If he is our light, what is there to fear about nighttime? Listen to the psalmist as he sings praise for God's very personal care:

> Even the darkness is not dark to you;
>> the night is bright as the day,
>> for darkness is as light with you. (Ps. 139:12)

Come into the Light

Those who know God in Christ have nothing to fear from nighttime. So it stands to reason that we ended up here, preferring our own means of escape, either because we don't believe or because we refuse to follow. And if we're refusing him, very likely, deep down inside our heart, it's because we resent him for failing to provide us what we've hoped for and think we need. He didn't provide a spouse; he didn't change our husband or save our wayward child. We feel that God let us down and therefore can't be trusted. So now, when 6:00 p.m. rolls around, we simply check out until morning. And we've been doing it for so long that we can't even see that we're living a double life:

> God is light, and in him is no darkness at all. If we say we have fellowship with him while we walk in darkness, we lie and do not practice the truth. (1 John 1:5–6)

When the apostle Paul wrote to the Thessalonian Christians, he exhorted them to be ready for the return of Jesus:

> For you are all children of light, children of the day. We are not of the night or of the darkness. So then let us not sleep, as others do, but let us keep awake and be sober. For those who sleep, sleep at night, and those who get drunk,

are drunk at night. But since we belong to the day, let us be sober, having put on the breastplate of faith and love, and for a helmet the hope of salvation. (1 Thess. 5:5–8)

His warning applies to us too. Do we want to be sin-numbed when he arrives? Of course not. If we've been united to Christ by faith, we belong to the day—even now, before he returns. So why do we spend a portion of each twenty-four-hour period as children of darkness? That's what we're doing when we depend on something—anything—besides the Lord to get us through the nighttime blues.

Yet we will turn away from our old, useless strategies only if we put on that armor of faith and love and hope. One way we cover ourselves with it is by being willing for God to meet us in our loneliness in a manner different from what we've wanted. If we will do that, we will find sooner or later that nighttime is no longer scary. We won't be paralyzed anymore by what to do with ourselves during those solitary evenings. In place of anxiety we will experience security:

It is in vain that you rise up early
   and go late to rest,
eating the bread of anxious toil;
   for he gives to his beloved sleep. (Ps. 127:2)

In the place of discouragement, we will know hope:

Light dawns in the darkness for the upright;
   he is gracious, merciful, and righteous. (Ps. 112:4)

On a practical level, if we're stuck when it comes to figuring out how to live life after sunset, here's the apostle Paul to get us started:

At one time you were darkness, but now you are light in the
Lord . . . Look carefully then how you walk, not as unwise
but as wise, making the best use of the time, because the
days are evil. Therefore do not be foolish, but understand
what the will of the Lord is. And do not get drunk with
wine, for that is debauchery, but be filled with the Spirit,
addressing one another in psalms and hymns and spiritual
songs, singing and making melody to the Lord with your
heart, giving thanks always and for everything to God the
Father in the name of our Lord Jesus Christ, submitting to
one another out of reverence for Christ. (Eph. 5:8, 15–21)

We begin by acknowledging our status—we may be alone in the
dark, but we ourselves are not dark. In the Lord we are light. If
all that sounds too abstract, we can ask him to show us what it
looks like practically. He will.

Change may take time, but we can begin right now, today.
We approach the end of the day "carefully," perhaps by acknowledging to God—and maybe a friend as well—our need
of divine aid to break old patterns and sinful coping strategies.
We ask God to kindle within us a passion to make "the best use
of the time" during those hours leading up to bed. At the same
time we begin to replace our old reliance on numbing activities
or substances with a renewed reliance on the Lord, allowing his
Spirit, whom we have quenched night after night, to fill us afresh
with fullness of joy. On a very practical level, Paul points out in
this passage the importance of fellowship, praise, and prayer. To
the degree that our old coping strategies have included sin is the
likely degree to which we have isolated ourselves from other believers. If we are lonely at night—and alone—could this be why?

Change will come as we take steps to interact with other believers. For some of us, being too tired to go out has really been

an excuse to stay home and get numb. If we are among those who truly cannot venture out after dark, we can nevertheless come into the evening "singing and making melody to the Lord with [our] heart." He is sufficient. If we will take Paul's words to heart and go forward, we will change even if our circumstances do not.

At the end of the day—literally!—God doesn't leave us to ourselves to get it right. The fact is, no matter what we do, we are going to have the occasional lonely night—or seasons of lonely nights—because we are fallen women living in a fallen world with other fallen people. And since that's true, the dread of night is likely to come at times and wrap around us like a cold blanket, even when we're doing all we can to walk as children of light. But it's right here that God comes in ways we didn't expect. He hasn't left us. In fact, we can be confident that he orchestrates our lonely times for good purposes.

Light in the Darkness

That is exactly what God did for the patriarch Jacob, who found himself alone one dark night—in part a consequence of his generally self-protective lifestyle. While he was alone, "a man wrestled with him until the breaking of the day" (Gen. 32:24). This man, who was likely the Lord himself, allowed the wrestling match to go on for some time before bringing about the outcome he intended: "When the man saw that he did not prevail against Jacob, he touched his hip socket, and Jacob's hip was put out of joint as he wrestled with him" (v. 25). The man wished to leave, but Jacob held tightly to him, demanding a blessing. In response, the man changed Jacob's name: "Your name shall no longer be called Jacob, but Israel, for you have striven with God and with men, and have prevailed" (v. 28). Jacob walked with a limp afterward, but it served to remind him who controls things. The divine encounter was a turning point in Jacob's life. And it happened while he was alone.

We aren't told how this "man" came to Jacob; suddenly he was just there. But it's safe to infer that he initiated the wrestling match. That's what God does—he comes to get us out of our troubles and primarily out of ourselves. That's what he did with Jacob that night—he brought him to the end of himself. Wrestling is a grueling sport (which is why regulated matches go on for only two or three minutes), yet Jacob's match went on until daybreak. The Lord could have ended the match victoriously at any point, of course, but he allowed it to continue. By this means Jacob was weakened but not broken, forced to yield yet held close. And in the Lord's perfect time, a breaking did occur so that Jacob was humbled. That was the Lord's goal all along—the humbling of Jacob.

Humility breeds dependence on God—or better said, it shows us just how dependent on him we are. Humility also changes our focus, turning us outward and upward rather than inward. In other words, humble people aren't self-consumed. Humility is also necessary for repentance, for apart from that we remain defensively protective of our rights and our excuses and our small self-justifications. As Peter wrote, "Clothe yourselves, all of you, with humility toward one another, for 'God opposes the proud but gives grace to the humble.' Humble yourselves, therefore, under the mighty hand of God so that at the proper time he may exalt you, casting all your anxieties on him, because he cares for you" (1 Pet. 5:5–7).

As a beloved pastor once told me, "God always breaks those he really plans to use." God had big plans for Jacob—plans that included the entire unfolding of his redemptive plan for all his people through Jacob's descendant Jesus Christ. So the breaking of Jacob was necessary, not only for Jacob's well-being but for the well-being of millions and ultimately for the glory of God. God has plans for you and me today as well, so he will break us too. And those lonely nights can be a place where he will meet us to bring it about. He wrestles us then, forcing us to cling to him in what we cannot ultimately escape or fix. In the process, we are mastered by him and further transformed into his likeness.

So when 5:00 p.m. approaches, we need not panic. We are not alone when the sun goes down.

• • •

Questions for Discussion or Reflection from Chapter 4

1. Why do you think nighttime is typically more difficult emotionally than daytime? Discuss how you spend your evening hours. What dictates your choice of activities?

2. Scripture uses the concepts of light and darkness to show us much about Christ and life in God's kingdom. What do you learn from the following sample passages?

   • John 1:1–5; 8:12; 12:44–46
   • Romans 13:12
   • 2 Corinthians 4:6
   • 1 Thessalonians 5:4–5
   • 1 Peter 2:9
   • 1 John 1:5; 2:8–9

3. Review Ephesians 5:8–21, where God's people are called "light in the Lord" (v. 8). From this passage, list the specific ways in which we are to let our light shine. Which terms in

this passage can we equate with darkness and which terms with light?

4. Review the story of Jacob's long night in Genesis 32. What was God after with Jacob, and how did God accomplish his purpose?

5. The Psalms provide comfort and help for our nighttime anxieties. Which of the following passages speaks most to you, and why?

   • Psalm 3:5–6
   • Psalm 4:8
   • Psalm 121:3–4
   • Psalm 127:1–2

God moves in a mysterious way
His wonders to perform;
He plants His footsteps in the sea
And rides upon the storm.

Deep in unfathomable mines
Of never failing skill
He treasures up His bright designs
And works His sovereign will.

Ye fearful saints, fresh courage take;
The clouds ye so much dread
Are big with mercy and shall break
In blessings on your head.

Judge not the Lord by feeble sense,
But trust Him for His grace;
Behind a frowning providence
He hides a smiling face.

His purposes will ripen fast,
Unfolding every hour;
The bud may have a bitter taste,
But sweet will be the flower.

Blind unbelief is sure to err
And scan His work in vain;
God is His own interpreter,
And He will make it plain.

—William Cowper, "God Moves in a Mysterious Way"

5

The Loneliness of Obedience

Colleen broke up with Jack. She knew it was right, but ending the relationship was the hardest thing she had ever done. Five years of togetherness. Five years of hoping and praying. But Jack had no real interest in Jesus. Oh, he'd come to church with Colleen, and he even attended a men's Bible study for a few months, but his heart was never in it. Colleen's friends could see what she could not—that Jack did those things only to keep peace with Colleen.

Colleen had finally come to understand the godly counsel she'd received throughout her years with Jack. "God calls us away from what compromises our devotion to him," she'd been told repeatedly. Yet rather than face this reality, Colleen had chosen to remain with Jack in hopes of his becoming a Christian. "I'm not giving up on him," she'd told her friends. "I have faith that God will change him." But Colleen hadn't understood until recently that clinging to Jack was not faith. It was disobedience. Accepting the truth gave her courage to end the relationship.

Colleen had another motivation for leaving Jack—she'd turned thirty-two. Desiring a family of her own, she had to face the fact that Jack might never become husband material, and therefore she should free herself for a godly man. So a few months after the breakup from Jack, once the grief abated, Colleen began to anticipate the future, and she threw herself into activities where she could meet a prospective husband. One or two men seemed promising initially, but neither prospect panned out, so after a few months, Colleen redoubled her efforts and joined a few Internet matchmaking sites. Nothing. No one.

• • •

Those were Colleen's reflections as she lay in bed the morning of her thirty-fifth birthday, a milestone she did not want to get up and face. Still single. No real prospects. Meanwhile, she'd learned two months earlier that Jack had gotten married. Why hadn't God blessed her? She'd been obedient. She'd placed herself in the right spiritual position. Now, at thirty-five, she was no closer to having her own family. She felt as though God had let her down, leaving her alone and lonely, and she resented it.

What Did We Expect?

Before we pass judgment on Colleen, let's ask ourselves whether we are really that much different. Have we ever obeyed God as a bargaining chip? That's exactly what's going on when our hope for blessing is rooted, as Colleen's is, in "placing ourselves in the right spiritual position." And sometimes it's not that we place ourselves there; life does it to us. A man breaks up with us, or we lose our job, or some other kind of difficulty takes us through a time of spiritual stretching, and we come to believe that as a result, some major, tangible blessing is right around the corner. When that doesn't happen, we so often wind up right where Colleen did—resentful.

The truth is, walking faithfully with the Lord leads sometimes to the very opposite of what we want. So we need to forget the idea that there's a direct correspondence between obedience and the earthly blessings we so much hope for. Jesus himself cautioned would-be disciples to count the cost of following him, because there would indeed be a cost. Sometimes that cost is loneliness. Are we willing for that, or will we resent God and turn away in unbelief? It all depends on why we've been following him in the first place.

The day after Jesus miraculously fed five thousand people, a large number of them sought to follow him, but he said to them: "You are seeking me, not because you saw signs, but *because you ate your fill of the loaves*" (John 6:25–26). When the trials and tests of faith hit and our dreams don't seem to be coming true, it's often then that we'll know if we treasure him for who he is or for what we've been hoping he'll do for us. If we resent how he has ordered our life, we can be sure we've been following him for the wrong reasons.

The Cost of Obedience

We can benefit from thinking about Joseph at this point, especially as we see him in Genesis 39, where we find him working as overseer in the house of an Egyptian official named Potiphar. Up to this point, the circumstances of Joseph's life had been largely dictated by others. His brothers had sold him to slave traders who had brought him down to Egypt, where he was purchased by Potiphar. Nevertheless, we are told, "the Lord was with Joseph" (v. 2). Ultimately, man was not dictating Joseph's life; God was. And the Lord blessed Joseph by giving him great success in his endeavors, such that his reputation and responsibilities grew greater.

But Joseph's climb to the top came tumbling down, once again through the actions of others—this time, a woman. Potiphar's wife lusted after Joseph and tried to seduce him. Day after day she made her appeal, yet Joseph continually rebuffed her, saying, "Behold, because of me my master has no concern about anything in the house, and he has put everything that he has in my charge. He is not greater in this house than I am, nor has he kept back anything from me except you, because you are his wife. How then can I do this great wickedness and sin against God?" (Gen. 39:8–9). But she persisted, and finally her verbal appeals became physical. She grabbed Joseph's clothing one day and tried to pull him into a sexual encounter. But Joseph tore away from her and ran out of the house. In the proverbial fury of a woman scorned, Potiphar's wife claimed that Joseph had tried to molest her, and as a result Joseph was thrown in prison.

Can we not see clearly here that obedience to God isn't necessarily a straight path to tangible blessing? It certainly wasn't for Joseph. He went from trusted servant to despised prisoner, and there's no doubt that the prison to which he was sent lacked court-appointed defense attorneys and cable television. To the contrary, we're told in Psalm 105 that "his feet were hurt with fetters," and "his neck was put in a collar of iron" (v. 18). And all this *because* he obeyed God.

Nevertheless, "the LORD was with Joseph and showed him steadfast love and gave him favor. . . . And whatever he did, the LORD made it succeed" (Gen. 39:21, 23). In time, Joseph was given the care of two men in the prison—royal officials who'd been banished from the administration for displeasing their ruler, Pharaoh. By means of a divine gift, Joseph was enabled to interpret the dreams of these imprisoned officials, asking only in return that the one soon to be released would afterward come to Joseph's aid. But despite Joseph's request, the released prisoner "did not remember Joseph, but forgot him" (Gen. 40:23). Joseph would languish in prison two more years before the Lord orchestrated his release and began to unfold a powerful redemptive plan in which Joseph was to play a primary role.

How did Joseph fare during this time? We aren't told what he thought or felt; all we know is that he survived it. We can be sure, however, that loneliness was a dominant theme in his heart, as evidenced from the fact that he was forgotten, not remembered. Being forgotten is always lonely, which is why some people dread their birthday. Better no birthday at all than to have it forgotten by those who matter to us. We tell ourselves it's a little thing—and, really, it is! If we'd just get our eyes off ourselves and onto others, it wouldn't matter at all. We know that's true! And we so much don't want it to matter. Yet it still stings, and that sting is the loneliness of being forgotten.

There's really no comparison between a forgotten birthday and Joseph's plight. The point is, he was lonely. He'd been mistreated by so many and then cast off and forgotten by others. Perhaps Joseph was tempted during this dark time to attribute those same things to God. We don't know what went through his mind; we're told only that "the word of the LORD tested him" (Ps. 105:19). Yet although we aren't told much about Joseph's state of mind, we know the Lord was with him every moment of every dark day and that he was directing everything and everyone to the end he intended. The fact of God's sovereign and loving presence is evident to us, but it likely wasn't always as clear to Joseph. Did he ever think how much easier it would have been to simply give in to Potiphar's wife? We don't know. What we do know is that he didn't give in. He resisted. He refused to sin against God, no matter the cost.

How different we are from Joseph! If we're honest, most of us have to admit we're a lot more like Colleen. We work to get our spiritual house in order by obeying God, but no big payoff results. In fact, our circumstances often seem worse afterward. When that happens, we so easily find ourselves grumbling or second-guessing our obedience. But that's the very point at which our faith is being tested. Do we obey God because we love him? Are we disciples because our passion has been captured by God's redemptive plans, not only for ourselves personally but for all his people? Because if it's primarily about what we get from him in the here and now, we will wind up disillusioned, unbelieving, and black-hole lonely.

Regardless of all that might have gone through Joseph's mind during his miserable imprisonment, he did not regret his obedience, and not only because he later became second-in-command over all of Egypt. It's because God's agenda was Joseph's agenda. In other words, Joseph saw everything that had happened to him as a means to advance God's plans and purposes, and he had embraced that as his own purpose. Just look at what he said to his brothers when they were finally reunited:

> Do not be distressed or angry with yourselves because you sold me here, for God sent me before you to preserve life. For the famine has been in the land these two years, and there are yet five years in which there will be neither plowing nor harvest. And God sent me before you to preserve for you a remnant on earth, and to keep alive for you many survivors. So it was not you who sent me here, but God. (Gen. 45:5–8)

No anger, no revenge—just a matter-of-fact statement about God's sovereign oversight and redemptive plan. It's likely that Joseph's deepest insight into the purposes of God were developed and established while his faith was being tested. God always has a redemptive purpose in the lonely seasons of his people, not just for the benefit of the lonely one but also for "many survivors." Lonely times are preparatory times, but we will be able to see this and embrace the goodness of it only if we make God's purposes our own. That's what Joseph did.

Yet the story of Joseph doesn't end with Joseph. He points us to someone else who was mistreated and suffered for his obedience—Jesus Christ.

The Greater Joseph

Like Joseph, Jesus was tempted. And like Joseph he resisted (see Matt. 4:1–11). But Jesus's resistance was also different. Unlike Joseph, Jesus resisted for us, on our behalf. His refusal to give in to temptation covers us when we do. Jesus's perfect obedience to the Father is applied to our imperfect, halfhearted, mixed-motive obedience.

On top of that, all Joseph's difficulties point forward to the trials Jesus experienced as a man. Joseph was able to free his brothers from self-recrimination over all they'd done by pointing them to God's bigger purpose, which found its ultimate fulfillment at the cross of Christ:

> There is therefore now no condemnation for those who are in Christ Jesus. For the law of the Spirit of life has set you free in Christ Jesus from the law of sin and death. For God has done what the law, weakened by the flesh, could not do. By sending his own Son in the likeness of sinful flesh and for sin, he condemned sin in the flesh, in order that the

righteous requirement of the law might be fulfilled in us, who walk not according to the flesh but according to the Spirit. (Rom. 8:1–4)

In Christ we are not condemned, and we have been set free to walk according to the Spirit. And because we're indwelt by the Spirit, we too, like Joseph, are now privy to God's overarching purposes—to preserve many people alive. Joseph was a short-term redeemer for a limited number of people, but the one he points to is a Redeemer for all people for all time through his life, death, and resurrection.

The redemption of many lives through the power of God—Joseph was on board with God's plan. The question is, are we? Colleen gave up something she wanted—a boyfriend—for something she wanted more—a husband. But her plan didn't work out as she'd hoped. She has a wrong understanding of how God works and what his purposes are, and because of that, today she is not only lonely; she is also bitter. She believes God let her down. Of course that's not true. God's agenda is just entirely different—and so much bigger. His plans for Colleen may include marriage. Whether they do or don't, God's plans for Colleen most definitely include bringing her into his big-picture work of redemption in a particular place with particular people. That doesn't mean she won't be alone at times, and no doubt there will be lonely seasons. But even then, if she will forsake her agenda and take up God's, she will find peace and fullness of life.

Obedience is never regrettable, and if God's purposes become ours, we will know that truth in our own experience. It's what Paul meant when he told us to offer ourselves to God as a living sacrifice—to let go of our own goals in order to participate in God's—and in so doing, we will find that what God does with our life is "good and acceptable and perfect" (Rom. 12:1–2).

• • •

Questions for Discussion or Reflection from Chapter 5

1. Jesus knows the hearts of those who follow him, as he demonstrated when he told some would-be followers, "You are seeking me, not because you saw signs, but because you ate your fill of the loaves" (John 6:25–26). What might he say to you in this regard?

2. How does our response to disappointment reveal our heart toward God? Provide an example from your own life as you ponder the life of Joseph in Genesis.

3. Where in your life has obedience proved costly? What did you learn in the process about God and about your heart for him?

4. Discuss the statement "Lonely times are preparatory times" (p. 67).

5. Read Romans 12:1–2. What does it mean to offer ourselves to God as a living sacrifice? What does Paul mean here when he says that conformity to Christ enables us to prove the goodness of God's will?

O Lord, you have searched me and known me!
You know when I sit down and when I rise up;
  you discern my thoughts from afar.
You search out my path and my lying down
  and are acquainted with all my ways.
Even before a word is on my tongue,
  behold, O Lord, you know it altogether.
You hem me in, behind and before,
  and lay your hand upon me.
Such knowledge is too wonderful for me;
  it is high; I cannot attain it.

Where shall I go from your Spirit?
  Or where shall I flee from your presence?
If I ascend to heaven, you are there!
  If I make my bed in Sheol, you are there!
If I take the wings of the morning
  and dwell in the uttermost parts of the sea,
even there your hand shall lead me,
  and your right hand shall hold me.
If I say, "Surely the darkness shall cover me,
  and the light about me be night,"
even the darkness is not dark to you;
  the night is bright as the day,
  for darkness is as light with you.

—Psalm 139:1–12

6

The Loneliness of
Running Away

"What are you doing here?" That's what the Lord asked Elijah
the prophet when he was hiding in a cave on Mount Horeb. The
implications were clear: Elijah was not where he was supposed
to be. God still comes with that question today. Has it come to
you lately? It won't come directly from the mouth of God, as
it did for Elijah; instead it will come through the lips of a close
friend or the conviction of the Holy Spirit as we're reading God's
Word. However it may come, we can be sure it will if we step
away from God's path.

Under a Broom Tree
So why was Elijah, the Lord's great prophet, all alone in that
cave, where we find him in 1 Kings 19? As with everyone who
winds up in the wrong place, Elijah's journey to the low point
of that cave was a process. And as is also so often true, it came

immediately after a high point. Just one month earlier, God had performed mighty miracles through Elijah's ministry, bringing about the defeat of Israel's enemies and a revival among God's people. But rather than securing for Elijah the adulation and prosperity that come to many high-profile ministers today, his ministry success proved personally costly.

Elijah had exposed the prominent idols of his day, the Baals, for what they really were—false gods—and the Baal worshipers were enraged, most especially Jezebel, the wife of Israel's king. She had devoted her energies as Israel's first lady to promoting those idols among the people. She was so angry that she vowed to have Elijah killed, and that's when we're told that "he was afraid, and he arose and ran for his life" (1 Kings 19:3). This mighty prophet who had held his ground against an entire mob of Baal worshipers fled in fear from one woman.

After a day of running, he was exhausted, so he sat down under a broom tree. Not only was Elijah afraid; he was also discouraged. The two often go together; in fact, one fuels the other. His tumultuous emotions are evident as he pours out his angst to God:

> He asked that he might die, saying, "It is enough; now, O LORD, take away my life, for I am no better than my fathers." (1 Kings 19:4)

Have you ever been so low that you wished for death? It's what sometimes happens when discouragement deepens to despair. "It is enough," he said. In other words, Elijah was done with serving the Lord. After all, where had it gotten him? Cowering under a tree, in fear for his life and all alone. Elijah's goal had never been fame or popularity or wealth; he simply wanted God's ways to triumph over wicked people and their ways. He thought this good goal had advanced with his defeat of the Baals, but given Queen Jezebel's threats, perhaps he'd been wrong about that. It seemed his great victory wasn't so great after all. Perhaps he was no more effective than the prophets who'd gone before him. So why bother anymore? "It is enough."

Some of us are sitting under a broom tree today because we too have said, "It is enough." We got there when we discovered that our child was the only one not invited to the neighborhood pool party because other parents don't want their kids associating with Bible thumpers. "If this is what happens for being forthright with the gospel in hopes of bringing the light of Christ to our sin-darkened neighbors, it's not worth it," we say. "I don't mind if they reject me, but my child—that's another story!" Or we got under the broom tree after seeing the Bible study we lead diminish in size despite our labors to prepare biblically sound lessons for the weekly meeting. Rumor has it that the ladies who no longer come are attending that new bells-and-whistles study group that's going through that trendy book. Or we got there when the young woman we've been discipling for hours and hours each month stays stuck in the same old destructive sin patterns.

What Are We Really Seeking?

What's the point? Why bother? It is enough. If we don't want to end up alone under a broom tree when we hit that point, or if we find ourselves already under one, there's something we've got to realize, and that's the likelihood that our discouragement and subsequent running away from serving God are rooted in wrong expectations. If we expect a one-to-one correspondence between effort and success, we are bound to be disappointed. Sometimes we get excited about the prospect because we see it happening for others. A pastor writes a book, and it's well received, so he's encouraged to write another and then another. Before long, he has become a "brand," and he's urged to cultivate his brand by cranking out more books and blog posts. When his following reaches a certain size, he then has a well-established "platform," which leads to more lucrative publishing deals and speaking gigs. Just scroll through the Twitter feeds of many popular Christian authors, and you'll find tweets like these:

> Here's a link to my take on . . .

> My new article is up and running at . . .

> Honored to be chosen for . . .

> You can find my speaking schedule at . . .

We think of that as success, but is it really? It all depends on how we define the term. The apostle Paul defined it with these words he penned while imprisoned:

> It is my eager expectation and hope that I will not be at all ashamed, but that with full courage now as always Christ will be honored in my body, whether by life or by death. For to me to live is Christ, and to die is gain. (Phil. 1:20–21)

And with these words:

> Indeed, I count everything as loss because of the surpassing worth of knowing Christ Jesus my Lord. For his sake I have suffered the loss of all things and count them as rubbish, in order that I may gain Christ and be found in him, not having a righteousness of my own that comes from the law, but that which comes through faith in Christ, the righteousness

from God that depends on faith—that I may know him and
the power of his resurrection, and may share his sufferings,
becoming like him in his death, that by any means possible
I may attain the resurrection from the dead. (Phil. 3:8–11)

I encountered a young woman a few years ago who had just
finished writing her first book. Her excitement was palpable
as she anticipated all the ways her life might change as a result
of getting published by a reputable Christian publisher. A few
months later, the book was released, and while the feedback was
positive, the book didn't become a best seller. In fact, reception
was modest, and I cannot recall hearing anything further about
it after its first season in print. I do recall, however, this young
author expressing on social media shortly thereafter bewilder-
ment and disappointment that it hadn't launched her life into
the hoped-for place of her dreams.

When disappointment comes, we will find out what was
motivating our ministry efforts in the first place. Is it the Lord
we've been serving or our own personal hopes? Have we been
zealous for spreading God's fame or for carving out a certain
identity? And if we have known a measure of success, does the
taste of it compel us to acquire more? Do we continue to churn
it out because we're afraid of fading back into obscurity? If we
find ourselves alone under a broom tree, we might want to give
it some thought.

Well, God doesn't abandon us to our broom trees, as we see
with Elijah. An angel was sent to refresh him and prepare him
to get back up and continue on. Even when we run away from
serving God, he doesn't run away from us. If we are in union
with Christ, nothing can snatch us out of his hand (John 10:28)
or make him turn his back on us (2 Tim. 2:13)—not our discouragement, not our fear, not even our running away.

When We Get It Wrong

Elijah continued on his way to Mount Horeb, but it's clear that his outlook hadn't changed much, because he merely exchanged the broom tree for a cave. He was still on the run. And all alone. Running away from our life—the one God marks out for us— always intensifies loneliness and isolation. What a mercy that God never changes! His plans for us do not change, nor do his intentions to bring us back. That's why Elijah heard the same question he'd heard forty days earlier under the broom tree: "What are you doing here, Elijah?" (1 Kings 19:9).

Elijah then did something we all tend to do when we're confronted with the truth about ourselves—he got defensive. He said, "I have been very jealous for the LORD, the God of hosts. For the people of Israel have forsaken your covenant, thrown down your altars, and killed your prophets with the sword, and I, even I only, am left, and they seek my life, to take it away" (1 Kings 19:10).

He tried to justify his running. He pointed out how much of himself he'd poured into serving the Lord and how very little his efforts seemed to have paid off. Rather than taking the long view, he was fixated on short-term results. There we see another factor in our own discouragement. If we're frustrated when the Internet is slow or excessively irritated by the full-basketed shopper in the express lane, then it's pretty likely that we're going to be discouraged if our ministry efforts don't soon bear visible fruit. We're an instantaneous people, and we carry that expectation into every area of life. But God doesn't work that way, as a close look at his work through redemptive history will reveal. When it comes to results, serving God faithfully means serving him blindly. We may never see the fruit of our prayers or our teaching or our writing or our godly parenting or whatever form our calling takes. If getting tangible results is our prerequisite for service, at some point we are bound to give up. We will only keep going if we do as Paul instructed: "Whatever you do, work heartily, as for the Lord and not for men" (Col. 3:23).

Although Elijah didn't live in a guaranteed-results culture like ours, he was caught up in short-term thinking, and it skewed his view of everything. "I, even I only, am left," he complained. That just wasn't true. Elijah was far from being the only remaining Israelite who despised false gods and sought their destruction. His discouragement warped his perspective, making him feel a lot more alone than he actually was. What's so ironic is that *Elijah truly isolated himself to escape what was merely the illusion of being isolated.* That's where we are going with all this. When we run away from God's call, we take ourselves away from God's people and from conscious enjoyment of the fellowship of God himself. Whether we run because the going gets rough, or because our expectations aren't met, or because we're secretly envious of others' success, or because our perceptions are skewed by discouragement, the outcome is the same—loneliness.

Could there be some of this in our lonely situation today? It's not always easy to see, and unwarping warped thinking is often a process, but if we turn to God, we can be sure we will find our way back. That's what happened to Elijah. When God came with his question, Elijah answered, pathetic though it was, and things began to turn around. God meets us where we are and reveals himself, just as he did for his self-pitying prophet.

After Elijah complained, God instructed the prophet to leave the cave and go stand on the mount before him, and this is what happened:

The LORD passed by, and a great and strong wind tore the mountains and broke in pieces the rocks before the LORD, but the LORD was not in the wind. And after the wind an earthquake, but the LORD was not in the earthquake. And after the earthquake a fire, but the LORD was not in the fire. And after the fire the sound of a low whisper. (1 Kings 19:11–12)

God was showing his prophet an important truth: earth-shattering events and spectacular displays, whether in nature or in our own callings, are not necessarily direct manifestations of God's presence and power. Sometimes, perhaps quite often, his presence and power are hidden in the things we consider small and insignificant. God is pleased at times to reveal himself in quietness.[7]

Afterward Elijah went and stood at the entrance of the cave, and God repeated his question: "What are you doing here, Elijah?" (1 Kings 19:13). Despite the miraculous nature show to which the prophet had been privately treated, he gave the same reply as before. "I have been very jealous for the LORD, the God of hosts . . ." blah, blah, blah. Even so, God didn't give up on him. He didn't wait for Elijah to get himself together. Instead, God called him out of the misery of his own making: "Go. Return on your way" (vv. 14–15).

The Way Back

The story of Elijah isn't really about Elijah. It's about God and who he is for his people—for us. We run away from his call. We complain. We try to hide from God, and we do hide from fellow believers. Where does it get us? Lonely and alone. If we see ourselves here, we need to quit listening to ourselves, to the self-talk that's keeping us stuck, and listen to God and all he says to us in his Word. But even if we fail in that regard, he doesn't leave us where we are. He comes calling: "What are you doing here?" Then he shows us afresh where we can find him, and he directs us back to pick up where we left off when we started running.

The story of Elijah is ultimately about Jesus, who was to come "in the spirit and power of Elijah" (Luke 1:17). Despite his failings, Elijah was indeed a great prophet—the most renowned of all in the Old Testament. Yet what made him so great had nothing whatsoever to do with his own efforts or even his own person. Elijah's greatness had everything to do with the One he unknowingly pointed to—the final and only sinless prophet, Jesus Christ. Whereas Elijah forsook his mission and ran from God, Jesus fulfilled his mission, even when he knew there'd come a day when God, however briefly, would run from him. Whereas Elijah complained in self-pity even while eating angel's food, Jesus was oppressed and afflicted, "yet he opened not his mouth" (Isa. 53:7). In all ways, Jesus was everything Elijah failed to be.

Jesus is the reason we too can get up and go back to our calling and the fellowship of those in it with us, because getting it right and producing results aren't the mission. Our call is to point to the only One who did get it right. It's Christ who's building his kingdom, not we.

• • •

Questions for Discussion or Reflection from Chapter 6

1. "What are you doing here?" When have you heard that question, and how did it come to you?

2. Review 1 Kings 19 (and also read the events that precede it in 1 Kings 18). Describe how these events influenced Elijah's thinking and brought him to discouragement.

3. Describe your current calling, whether a job, service in the church, raising a family, or a combination of things. What about your calling brings you joy? What tempts you to discouragement? Explain why in each case.

4. Have you ever run away from your calling? If so, how, and what happened? What restored you to it? If you are still running, what truths about God from the story of Elijah most inspire you to go back and take it up again?

5. What led Elijah to think he was all alone when he really wasn't? Can you identify similar thinking in your own life?

O heart bereaved and lonely
Whose brightest dreams have fled
Whose hopes like summer roses
Are withered, crushed, and dead,
Tho link by link is broken
And tears unseen may fall,
Look up amid thy sorrow
To him who knows it all.

O cling to thy Redeemer,
Thy Savior, Brother, Friend.
Believe and trust His promise,
To keep you till the end.
O watch and wait with patience,
And question all you will
His arms of love and mercy,
Are round about thee still.

Look up, the clouds are breaking,
The storm will soon be o'er
And thou shall reach the haven,
Where sorrows are no more.
Look up, be not discouraged;
Trust on, whate'er befall
Remember, O remember,
Thy Savior knows it all.

—Fanny Crosby, "He Knows It All"

7

The Loneliness of Grief

Grief is a solitary experience. No one else can feel exactly what you feel, even when the source of the pain is shared by others. Grief varies in intensity too, not just person to person but experience to experience.

Several years ago I lost a precious pet. My grief was real, and it was compounded by loneliness because I felt I had to hide the depth of pain I felt about the death of an animal. A decade later my father died, and I experienced grief at a whole new level. For weeks after, it ebbed and flowed like an ocean tide, and when the waves came, they poured over me with such force that I struggled to breathe.

When the End Comes

What makes grief so very, well, *grievous* is the finality of it all. Phil Ryken puts it well:

> Everyone carries a burden. It could be the death of a father
> or mother, brother or sister—something we think about

every day. It could be the death of a dream—something we hoped would happen, but now we know never will. It could be the death of the family we thought we had, but now everything has come undone. Grief is the pain of knowing life will never be the same.[8]

When that finality is the death of a loved one, we must face the fact that never again, in this lifetime at least, will we share a conversation, a simple pleasure, or a oneness with the one who's gone. And we anguish for how we took all that for granted when we had it. More painful still is the realization that the time has ended for fixing what was broken. All relationships are tainted by brokenness in one way or another because all of us are tainted by sin. Worst of all are the guilt-ridden thoughts that demand a place in our overburdened heart. The hurtful remarks we wish we'd never said; the selfish things we wish we'd never done; the requests for help we refused to heed—no one can fix this for us. No kind words can erase the past. We are alone in our pain.

Grief Compounded

That most surely was the case for King David following the tragic death of his son Absalom. Their relationship in the years leading up to the fateful day had not been good. In fact, it couldn't have been much worse. Absalom, disgruntled by his father's leadership, had decided to snatch the kingship away from David and claim it for himself. Absalom's efforts proved unsuccessful; nevertheless, he succeeded in driving David into hiding, in fear for his life. Despite Absalom's wicked intentions, David had a father's heart, and he loved his son; so when the final showdown was immanent and David's army was preparing to go to battle against Absalom's men, David ordered his commanders, "Deal gently for my sake with the young man Absalom" (2 Sam. 18:5).

David waited at home in the city for news from the battle-front. Certainly he desired victory for his army, but even more, he wanted his son, even on the enemy side, to be spared. So he waited anxiously. News finally came, and David's greatest fear was realized—Absalom was dead. David departed quickly to his private chamber, pouring forth as he went, "O my son Absalom, my son, my son Absalom! Would I had died instead of you, O Absalom, my son, my son!" (v. 33).

Surely in David's thoughts were memories of earlier times, of Absalom as a little boy, as a teenager—the good years before the trouble began. Surely he thought too of his own failings as a father, of which there had been many—his moral failings, lived out before his children, and his sometimes passive approach to parenting when sibling crises necessitated strong fatherly action (see 2 Samuel 13). And now there would never be a chance to make it right, to get the relationship back on positive footing. No, his son had died estranged from his father.

Compounding the awful pain of loss was the condemnation heaped on David by others for grieving over one who had become a national enemy, leaving him without any human consolation. His commander Joab came to his house and told him:

> You have today covered with shame the faces of all your servants, who have this day saved your life and the lives of your sons and your daughters and the lives of your wives and your concubines, because you love those who hate you and hate those who love you. For you have made it clear today that commanders and servants are nothing to you, for today I know that if Absalom were alive and all of us were dead today, then you would be pleased. (2 Sam. 19:5–6)

After issuing the rebuke, Joab advised him to paint a smile on his face and go out to greet his servants, because, he said, "if you do not go, not a man will stay with you this night, and this will be worse for you than all the evil that has come upon you from your youth until now" (2 Sam. 19:7).

David heeded Joab's words and went out to sit before his people, surely the loneliest hour of that grim day. No doubt David experienced the truth that loneliness is sometimes way more intense in a crowd than in solitude. When we are compelled to hide our pain, whatever the reason, we feel cut off from the world around us. Completely alone.

The loneliness is further intensified when we become aware that our grief is making some of those around us uncomfortable. They don't know what to say, and many feel the compulsion to try to fix our pain. Author Nancy Guthrie, who has grieved the loss of two children, understands the awkwardness:

> Even if you come up with the perfect thing to say (as if there is such a thing), it simply won't fix the hurt or solve the problem of the people who are grieving. . . . Really, there is nothing you can say that will make their loss hurt less. It's going to hurt for a while. They're not looking to you to make sense of it or to say something they haven't thought of or something that makes it not hurt. You purpose in saying something is to enter into the hurt with them and let them know they are not alone.[9]

The Man of Sorrows

That's all we really long for in our grief—to know we are not alone. Yet our loneliness is only compounded when we hear the well-intended but untruthful platitude, "Time heals all wounds." Time might bury the wounds, but it doesn't heal them. Only

Jesus can do that, which is why, in the loneliness—the helplessness—of grief, he is the one to turn to. In him we find a companion in suffering unlike any fellow human being can provide. First, Jesus understands our pain because he himself was "a man of sorrows and acquainted with grief" (Isa. 53:3). And his kind of understanding is way more than the small measure of comfort we get when someone empathizes, "Oh, I can relate to that. I've been where you are." Actually, there is little comfort when we hear that, because mentally we're screaming back, "No you haven't!" It's different with Jesus, because he actually knows our personal pain. "Surely he has borne our griefs and carried our sorrows" (Isa. 53:4).

When he paid for our sin on the cross, he bore the weight of its consequences too—every sorrow and every broken thing for every one of his people. It's beyond our comprehension, but it's true. He knows us personally, and his knowledge includes a comprehension of what each of us uniquely feels. We are not alone after all.

Have we turned to him in the loneliness of our own grief? If not, perhaps it's because, at some level, we wonder how we can find comfort in the One who had the power to prevent the loss in the first place. That's exactly how Mary and Martha felt after the death of Lazarus. "Lord, if you had been here, my brother would not have died," they said (John 11:21, 32). And even though Jesus knew the joy he was about to bring to these two sisters, he felt their heartbreak: "When Jesus saw [Mary] weeping . . . he was deeply moved in his spirit and greatly troubled. . . . Jesus wept" (vv. 33, 35). He doesn't merely sympathize with us—his heart breaks along with ours. That's what real love does, but *only* real love is able to do that.

One day several years ago, a business colleague left our office abruptly. Her sister, who'd been suffering a bad case of the flu, had just been taken to the hospital because her condition had dramatically worsened. My colleague and I had a solid working relationship, but we weren't close friends at that point, so I merely said a quick prayer for her and got on with my work. A few hours later I learned from my coworkers that my colleague's sister had died. The shock we all felt was understandable— relatively young women in well-developed countries don't typically die of the flu. What I didn't understand at first was the grief I felt. I closed my office door and wept for her loss and for her pain. With sudden clarity I realized that my emotional outpouring was an indicator of love. Somewhere along the way, she had become more than a colleague; she had become my friend.

Jesus is our friend. And he loves us so much more than we love one another. How much more, then, does he grieve for our grief? He is never uncomfortable with our pain. He never rebukes us when we can't seem to get past it. He lingers there with us, offering himself for our comfort. Because he is there, we are not alone in our grief.

• • •

Questions for Discussion or Reflection from Chapter 7

1. Describe your most painful experience of grief. How did loneliness factor in? Do you know why?

2. Discuss the factors that intensified David's grief over the loss of his son Absalom. Can you identify with any of these factors?

3. Isaiah 53:3–4 points to Jesus as "a man of sorrows and acquainted with grief." As you recall what you know of his

life from the Gospel accounts, describe specific incidents that fulfill Isaiah's prophecy.

4. Reread the story of Lazarus in John 11. What triggered Jesus's emotional display of sorrow? How did he comfort Mary and Martha?

5. "That's all we really long for in our grief—to know we are not alone." Discuss that statement from page 86.

O sacred head, now wounded,
with grief and shame weighed down,
now scornfully surrounded
with thorns, your only crown.
O sacred head, what glory
and blessing you have known!
Yet, though despised and gory,
I claim you as my own. . . .

What language shall I borrow
to thank you, dearest Friend,
for this, your dying sorrow,
your pity without end?
Lord, make me yours forever,
a loyal servant true,
and let me never, never
outlive my love to you.

—Isaac Watts, "O Sacred Head Now Wounded"

8

The Loneliness of
Being Different

The waiting room at the doctor's office was full and noisy. I had planned to use the wait time to catch up on some mandatory reading, but I was unable to concentrate. Remembering the two empty chairs I'd seen in the hallway just outside the door, I took my belongings out there and resumed my reading. A few minutes later a man walked by and entered the waiting room, only to come back out almost immediately and take the seat beside me. *Ah, another reader*, I thought. But he had no book. Nor did he have a cell phone. He just sat. Moments later, I was startled when the man's body jerked violently, emitting a loud snort in the process. I pretended I didn't notice. Not thirty seconds later, another violent jerk and snort, followed by another and then another. With sudden clarity, I realized why he had left the waiting room for the solitude of the hallway. Although overwhelmed with compassion for the man, I didn't know how to respond. I dared not look at him, and although we were only inches apart, he did not look over at me. While I had come out to the hallway for some peace and quiet, he had come out to avoid the revolted stares of a full waiting room. I could do nothing but pray for him, which I did. I tried to catch his eye with a smile before I left the hallway, but he wouldn't look at me. What a lonely life!

Cast Out

Being different—especially in a way that offends the sensibilities of others—surely breeds loneliness of the deepest kind. For some the cause is an illness, as with the man at the doctor's office. Others are born with deformities or are disfigured in an accident. And for many so afflicted, there will be no remedy in this lifetime. Where is God in this?

While we cannot know all his purposes in such cases, his Word reveals some of them, and through an ailing woman in Mark's Gospel we are shown his primary purpose. The story of this woman is found in Mark 5:25–34. She had a gynecological malady, and it had plagued her for twelve long years. She'd sought all possible medical help but to no avail. Her condition only worsened, and her suffering increased. Worst of all, perhaps, was the social suffering. Her condition resulted in an endless flow of blood, which in those days rendered her unfit for regular fellowship. Others saw her as unclean, and she was commanded by law to apply that label to herself. Adding insult to injury, anyone who had contact with her was, according to the law, rendered unclean as well:

> If a woman has a discharge of blood for many days, not at the time of her menstrual impurity, or if she has a discharge beyond the time of her impurity, all the days of the discharge she shall continue in uncleanness. As in the days

of her impurity, she shall be unclean. Every bed on which she lies, all the days of her discharge, shall be to her as the bed of her impurity. And everything on which she sits shall be unclean, as in the uncleanness of her menstrual impurity. And whoever touches these things shall be unclean, and shall wash his clothes and bathe himself in water and be unclean until the evening. But if she is cleansed of her discharge, she shall count for herself seven days, and after that she shall be clean. (Lev. 15:25–28)

Command the people of Israel that they put out of the camp everyone who is leprous or has a discharge and everyone who is unclean through contact with the dead. (Num. 5:2)

Clearly, her condition was not conducive to a dynamic social life. In fact, it basically kept her from having a social life at all for more than a decade. No doubt that was among the worst aspects of her illness.

The Blessing of Desperation

Despite her isolation, she had heard about Jesus, a man who reportedly could heal disease with merely a word and a touch. So one day she slipped into a crowd of people who were watching for him. Hopeless and out of options, she mustered up the courage to reach out and touch him as he passed by, hoping no one—least of all Jesus himself—would notice. "If I touch even his garments, I will be made well," she said (Mark 5:28). Sometimes, desperation is the door through which faith enters. "And immediately the flow of blood dried up, and she felt in her body that she was healed of her disease" (v. 29).

Jesus was aware that healing power had gone out of him, so he stopped in his tracks. "Who touched my garments?" he asked (v. 30). Did he not know? Most likely he did know, but he wanted the woman to come forward. He was issuing an invitation and preparing not only the woman but also the entire crowd to learn something about faith.

Terrified to the point of falling down, she came forward nevertheless. After all, if a mere touch of his cloak had healed her, surely it was safe to approach! So she revealed herself to him and told her story. When Jesus heard what had happened, he said, "Daughter, your faith has made you well; go in peace, and be healed of your disease" (v. 34). That's the last we read about her, but given the Jewish customs of the day, we can safely guess that afterward she went through the required purification rituals and was then restored to full fellowship within her community.

She was healed. She was made clean. She was restored.

"I believe that," you might be thinking, "but it doesn't happen that way for the majority of suffering people. So how does this show me where God is in the things that isolate me?" But actually, it *does* happen. This is exactly what God does for all who come to him by faith: he heals, he cleanses, and he restores.

Healed, Cleansed, and Restored

Our problem isn't God's failure to heal—it's our expectation of what that healing should look like. Often he does not give physical healing, although he could. But he always provides spiritual healing. And it's precisely at this point that we learn God's primary purpose in allowing the woman in Mark's Gospel to be afflicted in the first place—he wanted to heal her of sin and eternal separation from God. And God used her illness and the social isolation that came with it to bring that healing about. The physical healing she received was temporary, for this life only, but her spiritual healing was given for eternity. The flow of blood ceased, removing the disgrace of being socially unclean, but that too was temporary, because in those days before the death and resurrection of Christ, ritual cleansing was an ongoing necessity in the lives of God's people. That's why the cleansing she received from Jesus points to something so much greater—the cleansing that comes by being washed in his very own blood:

> When the goodness and loving kindness of God our Savior appeared, he saved us, not because of works done by us in righteousness, but according to his own mercy, by the washing of regeneration and renewal of the Holy Spirit, whom he poured out on us richly through Jesus Christ our Savior, so that being justified by his grace we might become heirs according to the hope of eternal life. (Titus 3:4–7)

We tend to miss this big picture—spiritual healing forever—because we so badly want the little picture—relief from suffering right now. But what if God's big-picture purpose will best be accomplished by not removing the hated thing that tends to isolate us from others? How we answer reveals which one we want most.

"I want both," we say. "Why does it have to be either-or?"

That's where we get stuck, and because we're stuck, we focus all our energy on finding a remedy that will make us normal and lift us out of the loneliness that comes from being different. But when no remedy works, to our loneliness is added frustration and discouragement.

There is only one way out of that muck, but there *is* a way out, as the woman in Mark's Gospel shows us. It's to get near to Jesus. He is the only one who can give us what we really long for. He can certainly change our circumstances if he chooses. And he just might. But even if he doesn't, he won't leave us to ourselves and all alone. He will give us himself, and if we're willing to let him have his way with us and with our problems, we will find him to be exactly what he is—the One who fills up what is lacking. He wants us to know him this way, and sometimes leaving us where we don't want to be is the only way we find it. As has been said so truly, sometimes we don't know that God is all we need until God is all we have.

How Good It Is!

If the prospect of spiritual healing doesn't wow us enough to press ahead and touch his garment, as it were, that's only because we don't understand how sick we really are. No illness or accident mars us as much as sin, and sin is the ultimate source of every isolation. No matter our physical malady, our sin-sick hearts are most in need of healing. Jesus is the only one with the remedy, and the healing he provides begins from the moment we reach out to him, and it penetrates every broken area of our lives.

We miss so much if we fixate on what we need to fit into the world around us. We imagine how much better life would be *if only*, but even if those *if onlys* come to pass, they won't fulfill us the way we think they will. Only Jesus does that. If we're not convinced, it's because we haven't really tasted how good it is—how good *he* is. Once we do, we won't despise our differences anymore. We certainly don't have to like them, but if they linger, we can come to know a sweetness that we wouldn't trade for anything.

Are we willing? That's the real question. If we let him choose for us, we will find way more than we've been hoping for with all our striving.

A Love Story

Long ago there was a man who fell in love with a woman he'd never met. This man was a lover of beauty, most especially concerning music and poetry, and he developed quite a reputation for his work. The man and the woman exchanged letters for months, and a long-distance romance had blossomed in the process. Finally the day arrived when the two would meet. The man was both nervous and excited, having anticipated this event with great joy. When the woman saw him, however, the romance died. She told him, "If only I could say that I admire the casket as much as I admire the jewel it contains."[10]

The man—this lover of beauty—was not beautiful. In fact, he was exceedingly unattractive by customary standards, and because of that, his would-be lover rejected him. His heart was broken. After that, he never married. But in his lonely heartbreak, he found something greater, and what it produced in his life still glorifies God and blesses many today. The man was Isaac Watts, the great hymn writer.

In Jesus, the things that make us different—and lonely—don't have to be an ongoing source of misery. If we stop insisting on the answer we think we need and leave the outcome in his all-wise healing hands, we'll find way more than we ever expected. "He has made *everything* beautiful in its time" (Eccles. 3:11).

• • •

Questions for Discussion or Reflection from Chapter 8

1. Is there an aspect of your person or your life that makes you different from others? If so, how has it factored in to your loneliness?

2. Review the story of the sick woman in Mark 5:25–34. Why did her malady result in social isolation? Why do you think she dared to touch Jesus? Why did Jesus heal her?

3. Of what three things can we be sure when we turn to Jesus for healing? How do these three things happen?

4. Why does spiritual healing fail to wow us as it should? How do we change our outlook about it? Make your answers personal.

5. How did being different bless Isaac Watts and, through him, many others? Review his hymn that is provided at the beginning of the chapter.

Come, ye sinners, poor and needy,
Weak and wounded, sick and sore;
Jesus ready stands to save you,
Full of pity, love and power. . . .

Come, ye thirsty, come, and welcome,
God's free bounty glorify;
True belief and true repentance,
Every grace that brings you night. . . .

Come, ye weary, heavy-laden
Lost and ruined by the fall
If you tarry 'til you're better
You will never come at all. . . .

Let not conscience make you linger,
Not of fitness fondly dream;
All the fitness He requireth
Is to feel your need of Him.

—Joseph Hart, "Come, Ye Sinners"

9

The Loneliness of
Being Unclean

On the eastern shore of the Sea of Galilee there was once a small town named Gerasa. On the outskirts, close to the shore, were the tombs—a dismal and desolate place where the townspeople buried their dead. Yet the deceased weren't the only ones occupying this bleak acreage. A man lived there. The tombs were a fit dwelling for this man because in some ways he was dead even while he lived. Held under the oppressive power of "an unclean spirit," he avoided the townspeople, and those people had also given up on him (Mark 5:1–4). Oh, many had tried to help him, to restrain the outworkings of his inner demons, but to no avail. The evil that dominated him worked not only to isolate him from people but also to destroy his very being: "Night and day among the tombs and on the mountains he was always crying out and cutting himself with stones" (v. 5).

It's hard to imagine a more terrible existence, isn't it? We read that story in Mark's Gospel, and it seems so far removed from anything that goes on in our world. Yet actually there are many like this lonely man everywhere, even today. They are in our towns and schools. They are even in our churches, and in our very own homes. Perhaps we ourselves are like him. We don't recognize the presence of evil, because unclean spirits in our day and age—at least in developed Western countries like ours—rarely possess people in such an assertive way. When we think of demonic influence, what comes to mind is the force that turned Linda Blair into a supernaturally strong, head-spinning, green-vomiting monster in *The Exorcist*. But as some have said, Satan's best trick is to make people believe he doesn't exist, and once he's done that, we no longer recognize his work as just that—*his* work. Not for nothing does Scripture call him "the deceiver of the whole world" (Rev. 12:9).

Demons and Idols: A Match Made in Hell

Satan's chief work is to rob God of his glory, and he does this primarily by doing whatever it takes to blind the world to the one true Lord, Jesus Christ. Satan doesn't really care what we do or whom we worship, so long as it isn't Jesus. He will distract us however he can. That's why we know that he takes a special interest in the sin of idolatry.[11] An idol is anything or anyone we trust or depend on in such a way as to displace Christ's lordship from our heart. Giving ourselves to an idol, allowing it mastery over our lives, is the sin of idolatry. In our God-denying culture, idolatry goes by other names: addiction, codependency, disease, dysfunction. Whatever we call it, if we consider idolatrous behavior from a biblical perspective, we can see that demonic influence, working in tandem with our own sin nature, always underlies it.

The influence of demons in the sin of idolatry is evidenced in the fact that idolatry involves misplaced worship. An idolator becomes increasingly dependent on her idol because she believes that the idol has the power to meet her needs and satisfy her longings, so she builds her life around it, doing whatever is necessary, at any cost, to safeguard its preeminent place in her life. Can you see how this is the essence of worship?

We never make a conscious choice to become an idolator, but we do make the choice to indulge in what eventually leads us there. It happens gradually, as we turn repeatedly to something or someone other than God to meet a felt need or desire. Over time, a dependence is formed, whether for pleasure or escape, displacing God in the process. As Jesus said: "No one can serve two masters, for either he will hate the one and love the other, or he will be devoted to the one and despise the other" (Matt. 6:24). When an idol rules our heart, Jesus does not. Whatever master we serve is the one we really worship.

The influence of demons in the sin of idolatry is also evidenced—blatantly so—in what the apostle Paul told the Corinthians, warning them, "Flee from idolatry. . . . I do not want you to be participants with demons. You cannot drink the cup of the Lord and the cup of demons. You cannot partake of the table of the Lord and the table of demons" (1 Cor. 10:14, 20–21). The worship of false gods, which is undergirded by demons, has always been a temptation, even for God's people, as far back as the early days of the nation of Israel, when Moses said of them:

They sacrificed to demons that were no gods,
    to gods they had never known,
to new gods that had come recently,
    whom your fathers had never dreaded.

> You were unmindful of the Rock that bore you,
>> and you forgot the God who gave you birth.
>>> (Deut. 32:17–18)

Such is the nature of idolatry. It's there in the Sunday morning churchgoer who doesn't attend Wednesday evening Bible study because it would mean forgoing her nightly cocktail. It's there in the teenager who spends all her meager earnings on food, then locks herself in her bedroom to binge and purge. It's there in the financially overextended woman who seeks relief from the day's anxiety in the purchase of yet another new outfit. It's there in the disappointed wife who seeks what she's always hoped for in the beds of men other than her husband. Idolatrous worship. Unclean spirits.

Alone and Dying

We are not told how the man in Mark's Gospel came to be possessed by demons, and we have no way of knowing what, if anything, he had done to fuel the problem. We don't need to know, because the demons and even the man himself are not the primary point of the story. We know only that he was in bondage to evil and that it had left him utterly isolated.

Isolation is another indicator of the matchup between demons and idolatry, and it characterizes the life of an idol worshiper. Shame is one cause; we cringe inside at the prospect of having our sin exposed, so we hide. Isolation is also a way to avoid confrontation. An idolator doesn't want anyone interfering and threatening to take away her false god. We always fight to hang on to what we believe has the power to bless us. Idolators are blind to the fact that what they perceive as blessing is really bondage. As Peter wrote, "Whatever overcomes a person, to that he is enslaved" (2 Pet. 2:19). Is this where you find yourself today? If so, you're likely aware of this vicious cycle. The longer you hang on, the more isolated you get, although you often don't feel the loneliness because you think you have all you need through your idol. All of us—whatever our pet sin—can be so completely alone because of it yet blind to that reality. What's so ironic is the fact that, more often than not, the idolatry began as an attempt to escape the very thing it creates—loneliness. Idolatry is a breeding ground for loneliness.

The work of unclean spirits in a sin-bound idolator also includes self-destruction. Unclean spirits promote self-destruction, as we see in the lonely man at the tombs, who cut himself with stones. However it shows up in an individual life, idolatry works self-destruction; it is a hallmark of it. Idol worship destroys our bodies, our bank accounts, and our relationships.

We have no idea what the man at the tombs looked like, but it's a pretty safe guess that he wasn't pleasing to the eye. Uncleanness does that. The idols of drugs and alcohol mar the abuser's face over time—broken capillaries, discolored skin, lightless eyes—just as relational idols mar the idolator's personality. When a person becomes our god, we lose our sense of self; we conform our identity to his or her demands and expectations in order to keep the relational dynamics in place.

Jesus Has the Final Say

Whether a substance or a human being or something else altogether, idols wrap us in uncleanness of both the powers of darkness and our own sin. And when uncleanness is allowed to linger, it also skews our view of God. The man at the tombs saw Jesus as his tormentor rather than as his Savior (Mark 5:7). But this brings us back around to where we want to be, because, despite his skewed view, when the demon-possessed man saw Jesus from afar, "he ran and fell down before him" (v. 6). He ran *toward* Jesus, not away, and Jesus cleansed the man of the demons. Jesus is Lord of all. He has authority over every unclean spirit, whatever form that uncleanness takes, and *that* is the point of this story here in Mark's Gospel. Enslaving idols are no match for the Lord of the universe. They cannot stand before him; they lose their power.

Clean Clothes

Is there an idol in your life making you unclean? That's what sin does to us. Years ago I was caught up in an idolatrous relationship. I knew it displeased the Lord, but I chose to ignore that fact. I wasn't ready to let go of the so-called blessings I got from it. One night during this dark season, I had a dream—a vile dream in which I was brought close to a pile of something we don't talk about in polite company. I won't recount the vivid details; suffice it to say that I recognized that the dream was a parable of where I had taken my life and heart.

Can you relate to that? Maybe you can—if not because of some specific sin pattern in your present, maybe because of some uncleanness in your past. Sin leaves us dirty inside and out, and because of that, it isolates us from God and from the fellowship of others. That was the plight of Joshua the high priest in Zechariah's prophecy. In Zechariah's vision, Satan was making a spectacle of Joshua's sinful uncleanness. In fact, we are told that Joshua "was clothed with filthy garments" (Zech. 3:3). But Satan didn't get the last word. The Lord was present, and he said, "Remove the filthy garments from him." And then he said to Joshua, "'Behold, I have taken your iniquity away from you, and I will clothe you with pure vestments.' . . . So they put a clean turban on his head and clothed him with garments" (vv. 4–5).

Sin makes us unclean, and unrepentant sin is a gateway to unclean spirits. But Jesus cleanses us with the blood he shed on the cross to pay for our sin. He removes our dirty clothes and covers us with clean garments, thereby removing the guilt and shame of our spiritual filth. That's why Jesus is the hope—the only hope—for those of us caught in the isolating bondage of idolatry.

What Jesus did for the man in Mark's Gospel, he will do for us too. If even right now we are locked in the grip of an ugly entanglement, warped in our understanding, we don't have to stay there, isolated among the tombs. Jesus may seem far off, but he is not. We can run toward him with all our uncleanness, and he will cleanse us. That's what he did for the demon-possessed man who lay at his feet. The darkness that dominated that man was no match for the Light of the world.

The Restorer of All That's Broken

Afterward, when the townspeople heard what Jesus had done, they came to see for themselves, and what they saw astonished them. The man whom no one had been able to help, the man they'd both pitied and feared—and therefore shunned—sat there before them "clothed and in his right mind" (Mark 5:15).

Idols steal. They steal not only our affections, our relationships, and our health but also our sanity. That's why Jesus is the idolator's only remedy. How-to books, Twelve Step programs, and caring people can help restrain sin and the outworkings of evil, but they cannot deliver an idolator's heart. Only Jesus can do that, and only he can unwarp a warped mind.

Only Jesus can fully restore the relationships that got broken during our season of bondage. The fact that the demon-delivered man in Mark was found clothed indicates his fitness to reenter society and repair broken relationships and form new ones. His isolation was over.

Only Jesus can turn a sin-dominated heart that flees from him into the heart of a disciple who longs to follow. That's what he did for the man at the tombs, whose earlier plea that Jesus leave him alone turned into a plea to go with Jesus.

And only Jesus can give a formerly wasted life a brand-new calling with eternal significance. "Go home to your friends and tell them how much the Lord has done for you, and how he has had mercy on you," Jesus told him (Mark 5:19).

Some of us, even as we read, are still caught in the grip of some sin, lingering there among the tombs, and the forces of evil, unclean spirits, are ever ready to encourage our enslavement by means of isolation, self-destruction, and wrong thinking about God. Is this where you are today? If so, know that the ability to say yes to that question and face this truth is God's grace in your life. Why not get up right now and run to Jesus?

$$\bullet \ \ \bullet \ \ \bullet$$

Questions for Discussion or Reflection from Chapter 9

1. Review the story of the demon-possessed man in Mark 5:1–20. Describe what his life was like among the tombs.

2. From the Scripture passages referenced in chapter 9, discuss the link between demons and idolatry.

3. Can you identify idols in your life? If so, how have they "wrapped you in uncleanness"? How have they enslaved you? How has idol worship isolated you from others?

4. Read Zechariah 3:1–5. In the prophet's vision, what does Satan do, and how does God triumph over him?

5. How was the man in Mark's Gospel different after Jesus freed him? As you think about this, consider the ways in which your life will be different when you finally forsake your idols and experience the cleansing of Jesus. If you have already taken this step, describe how your life is different as a result.

All are not taken; there are left behind
Living Belovèds, tender looks to bring
And make the daylight still a happy thing,
And tender voices, to make soft the wind:
But if it were not so—if I could find
No love in all this world for comforting,
Nor any path but hollowly did ring
Where "dust to dust" the love from life disjoin'd;
And if, before those sepulchers unmoving
I stood alone (as some forsaken lamb
Goes bleating up the moors in weary dearth)
Crying "Where are ye, O my loved and loving?"—
I know a voice would sound, "Daughter, I AM.
Can I suffice for Heaven and not for earth?"

—Elizabeth Barrett Browning, "Consolation"

10

The Loneliness of Misplaced Love

Health professionals advise us to drink eight glasses of water a day. I don't know about you, but I struggle to consume that recommended amount. I manage to get it down, however, with a few hydro-enhancements: steaming hot with a lemon wedge, or flavored with a bit of carbonation, or spring-produced and dressed up in pretty packaging. I'm not blind to what underlies my consumption struggle: I am a spoiled American who has never experienced real thirst. Those who have to work for their water have no difficulty consuming plain old water. Unlike me, they are oblivious to weird tastes coming from the tap—assuming they even have a tap.

A Woman Scorned

When Jesus walked this earth, people drew their water from wells, and this daily task was no small chore, as a sufficient amount had to be drawn up for both people and livestock. Drawing the water was women's work, and in the hot desert climate of the Middle East, the daily trek to the well was typically done either early in the morning or in the evening, when temperatures were cooler (see Gen. 24:11). No doubt the water drawing was also a social time for the women as they made their way to the well and back each day, adding a pleasant aspect to an otherwise mundane and arduous task.

In Samaria, however, there was a woman who walked alone to the well; she went at noontime, the hottest part of the day, when none of the other women would be there.

She preferred to do her work in solitude, either to avoid the other women or to escape the reality that they wished to avoid her. Whichever it was (perhaps both), she was a lonely woman, made so by both birth and bad choices. First, she was a Samaritan, a class of people who were despised by Jews. Added to that was her scandalous relational history.

She was shunned by polite society, but not by the Lord Jesus. He set out to encounter her one noonday at Jacob's well in the town of Sychar, and he asked her to give him some water from her bucket. She was rather startled by his request and said to him, "How is it that you, a Jew, ask for a drink from me, a woman of Samaria?" (John 4:9). Jesus was indeed thirsty; his stop at the well that day had been preceded by a hot, dusty journey from Judea. But he was more concerned with her thirst than his own, and he knew that her thirst ran much deeper than what could be quenched by a bucket of water, so he invited her to ask for living water rather than liquid. He told her, "Everyone who drinks of this water will be thirsty again, but whoever drinks of the water that I will give him will never be thirsty again. The water that I will give him will become in him a spring of water welling up to eternal life" (vv. 13–14).

She liked the sound of that. "Sir," she said. "Give me this water, so I will not be thirsty or have to come here to draw water" (v. 15). She misunderstood, as we so often do. Our physical and emotional needs feel so close and so immediate that we miss the truth that our deepest need is spiritual. That's what he wanted her to realize, and it's what he wants us to realize also.

True Refreshment

We can all relate to the water imagery Jesus used here in his conversation with the Samaritan woman, and not simply because we need drink to survive. We can also relate because both food and drink are so easily used—or misused—to cope with the difficulties of life. It's likely that at one time or another, each of us has known the temptation to turn there for comfort or escape or the pleasure we can't seem to find elsewhere.

Because that's true, and because food and drink are so vital, biblical invitations to the gospel—our greatest need and the answer to our deepest cravings—are often portrayed in these terms. We see it, for example, in Isaiah:

> Come, everyone who thirsts,
> come to the waters;
> and he who has no money,
> come, buy and eat!
> Come, buy wine and milk
> without money and without price.
> Why do you spend your money for that which
> is not bread,
> and your labor for that which does not satisfy?
> Listen diligently to me, and eat what is good,
> and delight yourselves in rich food. (Isa. 55:1–2)

It's there also in the invitation to Lady Wisdom's feast:

> Wisdom has built her house;
>   she has hewn her seven pillars.
> She has slaughtered her beasts; she has mixed her wine;
>   she has also set her table.
> She has sent out her young women to call
>   from the highest places in the town,
> "Whoever is simple, let him turn in here!"
>   To him who lacks sense she says,
> "Come, eat of my bread
>   and drink of the wine I have mixed.
> Leave your simple ways, and live,
>   and walk in the way of insight." (Prov. 9:1–6)

Living water was the real need of the lonely woman at the well. She had a terrible thirst that she'd spent years trying to quench, but she could not, because she'd been trying to draw from a dry well. For that reason, she initially saw Jesus's offer of living water in merely physical terms. Jesus knew that, of course, so he took her to an uncomfortable place. He said, "Go, call your husband, and come here."

She replied, "I have no husband."

So Jesus went even deeper: "You are right in saying, 'I have no husband'; for you have had five husbands, and the one you now have is not your husband" (John 4:17–18). In other words, "You've been drinking the wrong water, and it hasn't quenched your thirst."

Good Water and Bad

Are we really that much different? Like the Samaritan woman, we seek to quench our thirst with what we perceive will bring us love and a bit of happiness, yet so often our attempts at satisfaction leave us desperately lonely instead. But that's not how the living water flows. Jesus met her at the well that day not to fill her craving for love, although, of course, he certainly did love her. His primary point wasn't really about her at all—it was about him.

When we're fixated on getting the sort of love we think we need, Jesus's invitation to drink living water just doesn't grip us. So often we're not gripped until we're made to see the comparative emptiness of our own life-dominating pursuit. Jesus's invitation is a call to fixate on him. And amazingly, when we do, we find the fulfillment we've been looking for all along—the kind that nothing else ever truly provides.

The Samaritan woman had cycled through five husbands. We aren't told what happened to end those marriages, whether she had abandoned the men or they her. Perhaps one or two of those husbands had died. We don't know, but we do know, given her current live-in boyfriend, that her moral standards were set pretty low.

Let's face it—many of us can see ourselves in this woman. We might not have had five husbands, but we understand the temptation to seek fulfillment in the love of a man or in the illusion of love that props up sexual relationships outside of marriage. Or perhaps we have had five husbands (or four, or three, or two). Maybe we've devoted decades of exclusive friendship to a particular man in hope that he will propose marriage one day, but he never does, so to whom else can we go at this point? It's too late to hope for something better. We never find living water in these relationships. They are dry wells, the kind that the Lord had in mind here:

> My people have committed two evils:
> they have forsaken me,

> the fountain of living waters,
> and hewed out cisterns for themselves,
> broken cisterns that can hold no water. (Jer. 2:13)

As I said earlier, the loneliest women I know are not single women. The loneliest are those in a difficult marriage, or those in a morally compromised relationship. How utterly alone a woman feels as she lies in the dark beside a man with whom she cannot share her heart or her thoughts. Yet even the best of marriages go through lonely seasons, which is why we will find the living water for which we yearn only in Jesus.

Do you believe that? Some of us have to admit that while we get "Jesus as living water" in principle, our personal comprehension of it has come up a bit short. If that's the case, could it be that we don't know *Jesus* as our living water because we've been looking to him to make our *man* into living water? The Samaritan woman had her sights set on what she wanted Jesus to *do* for her rather than what he wanted to *be* for her. "Sir, give me this water, so that I will not be thirsty or have to come here to draw water." The living water Jesus gives is not about improving our love life. It's about something so much deeper and richer and more satisfying. It is thirst quenching in a way that the love of a man—even the best, most godly man—can never, ever be.

Paradoxically, the deeper our craving for a man's love, the more elusive it becomes. Have you ever noticed that? Women who are desperate to be loved often drive away the very thing they so badly want. When it plays out that way, it's actually a blessing in disguise, because God never intended the love of a man to be a woman's thirst quencher. If we attempt to use it that way, it will leave us even more parched. Only Jesus is our living water.

A Drink of Living Water

Some of us even now are living like the Samaritan woman before she encountered Jesus—facing the heat of the day all alone. We go about our tasks in such a way as to avoid the whispers and averted eyes of those who know our circumstances, whether past or present. We feel uncomfortable in church on Sunday, and we decline invitations to small-group activities because the stigma of our relational brokenness makes us feel unfit for full participation in Christian fellowship. For this reason, we actually feel less lonely out in the world than inside the church. Or we believe that our place in the church is limited to the divorce-recovery group or the monthly luncheon for single mothers. Full-on participation in gatherings of "normal" Christians? Forget about it.

But it's to such as these that Jesus comes. He actually seeks us out, as he did the Samaritan woman, and offers us the living water of himself. "That is always the way it is in the spiritual realm," writes James Boice. "Jesus comes to us first. If we were left to ourselves, we would leave him sitting on the edge of the well forever. But he does not leave us to ourselves. Instead he comes to us. He asks the first question. He initiates the conversation. He uses all devices to break through to our hearts. Sometimes it is a question, sometimes a command, sometimes a chance remark made by someone else, but it is always from him."[12] And then, in union with him, we are no longer characterized by relational damage; the stigma is eradicated. "If anyone is in Christ, he is a new creation. The old has passed away; behold, the new has come" (2 Cor. 5:17).

In Christ we find a whole new identity—his identity becomes ours. As we drink this living water, we discover that our human relationships are losing the power to define us, and the illusion that they can fulfill us is beginning to evaporate. And we come to understand our real need—what causes our thirst—for the first time. It's not the love of a man that we've needed after all; it's being set free from thinking it was. It's not having our past bad choices erased from view; it's having them forgiven. It's not the removal of all our sin's consequences; it's God's grace redeeming those consequences for our good and for others to whom he will send us. It is as he told her:

> Whoever drinks of the water that I will give him will never be thirsty again. The water that I will give him will become in him a spring of water welling up to eternal life. (John 4:14)

That's what happened to the woman in Samaria. I think we can safely infer that she fell in love with Jesus that day, not primarily because of anything she said or did, but because Jesus went looking for her and found her. Because of that, she discovered what happens to all who look to him for life—the stigma of shame and sin and the loneliness they produce are left in the dust. We know this was true in her case, because *immediately*—not at some nebulous, hoped-for time in the future—she "left her water jar and went away into town and said to the people, 'Come, see a man who told me all that I ever did. Can this be the Christ?'" (vv. 28–29).

The one who had shunned and been shunned in return now ran toward people rather than away. She went to them bearing not fodder for gossip but good news for redemption from gossip. She came not with sexual scandal but with a foreshadowing of the scandal of the cross. She came not with self-focused humiliation but with Christ-focused joy. Those living waters were already welling up.

She fades from history after that, but she leaves us a threefold legacy. First, from both her life and her encounter with Jesus, we see that the love of a man will never quench our deepest thirst. Second, we see that in Jesus our relational sins of the past and our relational longings in the present don't have to define us. Finally, we see that drinking the living water that wells up to eternal life makes us Christ-centered, and that, in turn, produces joy, fosters love, and remedies loneliness.

• • •

Questions for Discussion or Reflection from Chapter 10

1. Review the story of the Samaritan woman in John 4:1–42. Why was this woman isolated? How did Jesus happen to meet her at Jacob's well?

2. How does the Samaritan woman misunderstand Jesus's offer of living water? Why does she misunderstand?

3. Why does Jesus refer to himself as "living water"? In other words, what does he want us to know about him?

4. Review Proverbs 9:1–6 and Isaiah 55:1–2. Why are God's invitations in Scripture so often put in terms of food and drink? Where else in Scripture is food and drink used to illustrate life in Christ?

5. Discuss this statement from page 116: "The deeper our craving for a man's love, the more elusive it becomes." Where have you seen this played out?

On my bed by night
I sought him whom my soul loves;
    I sought him, but found him not.
I will rise now and go about the city,
    in the streets and in the squares;
I will seek him whom my soul loves.
    I sought him, but found him not.
The watchmen found me
    as they went about in the city.
"Have you seen him whom my soul loves?"
Scarcely had I passed them
    when I found him whom my soul loves.
I held him, and would not let him go
    until I had brought him into my mother's house,
    and into the chamber of her who conceived me.
I adjure you, O daughters of Jerusalem,
    by the gazelles or the does of the field,
that you not stir up or awaken love
    until it pleases.

—Song of Solomon 3:1–5

11

The Loneliness of Marriage

There are lots of lonely wives. In fact, married women can be among the loneliest of lonely people. One reason is that no one expects a wife to be lonely. After all, isn't marriage supposed to be God's remedy for loneliness? That's what she believes, so her loneliness is compounded by guilt. And when she attempts to talk about her loneliness, she's admonished to count her blessings.

Perhaps you are one of those wives. If so, do you know why you are lonely? Trying to answer that question can be part of the problem, because sometimes loneliness has no logical, discernable cause. It's just there. One morning a dear friend called to talk, and during our conversation she shared her lonely feelings. As I listened, I thought, *How can you, a busy mother with a good marriage, possibly be lonely?*

At the time I hadn't done much thinking about this topic. Now that I have, I realize that women who are constantly surrounded by people, by family, are no less lonely than the rest of us. It's just that being perpetually in the company of others masks it. My friend was in touch with those feelings on one of her rare days of solitude, that empty ache that only God can fill and which will be fully resolved only when we are perfected in glory, back at home with the Lord for eternity.

Lonely Wives

Other women, however, are made desperately lonely by what actually goes on in their marriage. I think, for example, of Diane, whose husband guards what she eats like a watchdog, ready to pounce with a rebuke or a disappointed glance if she orders dessert at a restaurant or nibbles a cheese puff from the appetizer tray. "I married a thin woman because I want a thin wife," he reminds her. Constantly. The only time Diane's loneliness lifts is immediately after a social outing at which others complimented her appearance. For a few hours, at least, she basks in the warm glow of her husband's proud pleasure and approval. Would he love her if she gained ten pounds? "Of course!" he assures her. But in her heart she's not so sure. And the thought of having children terrifies her because of how it will change her figure. Diane lives every day with the loneliness of conditional love.

• • •

There is also Bella, whose husband has come home from work sullen and uncommunicative almost daily for the past six months. When she tries to draw him out, he says nothing is wrong, and if she persists, he becomes irritable. After a silent dinner, he either turns on the television or retreats into the solitude of his home office. She lies awake beside him at night, wondering if he's hiding something. Is he bored with the marriage? Is he having an affair? Is there a problem with the finances? Her mind obsessively searches for clues. He says nothing is wrong. He says it's all in her head. But she knows things are different. She *knows* it! This new "normal" is the loneliest experience of her life.

• • •

Then there's Anne, whose husband never cut the maternal apron strings. When it comes to holidays, vacations, and raising the kids, her overbearing mother-in-law always has her say and always gets her way. Anne lives in a state of constant frustration, and then she feels guilty for being uncharitable. After all, her mother-in-law did loan them money for a down payment on the house (even though the loan was conditioned upon the purchase being in close proximity to her own home). And, yes, even though her mother-in-law drops by, uninvited, for a lengthy visit several times a week, she is always willing to babysit at the last minute. Anne realizes that her mother-in-law isn't really the problem; it's her husband's unwillingness to see Anne's plight and ever take her side.

Just this past year Anne had been excited at the prospect of hosting Thanksgiving. All the holidays for each of the preceding nine years had been celebrated at the home of her mother-in-law. This year Anne's parents were coming in from out of state—a rare occurrence—so she finally had a plausible excuse to host a holiday at her own home. For the first time she was able to plan the menu, the decorations, and the family activities, and she did so with joyous enthusiasm.

Three days before Thanksgiving, Anne returned home from a run of holiday errands to discover a voicemail from her mother-in-law, informing her of a change. "I've just hung up from talking to your mother," she told Anne. "I called to tell her that I thought it would be better to have everyone here at my house for Thanksgiving dinner. After all, I've got a lot more space. I told your mother that I want to unburden you from holiday dinner responsibilities, since you'll be hosting your parents for the whole weekend. Of course, when I explained all that, your mother completely agreed. So I'll see you all here at four o'clock."

Anne stood by the telephone shaking with rage, and then she dialed her husband. "How dare she call *my* mother!" she complained in tears. "I was all set to do this, and now your mother has taken it away from me!"

"What's the big deal?" he responded. "It's just a meal."

Is the problem as clear to you as it is to me? The real source of Anne's trouble isn't her mother-in-law (although, let's face it—she's hardly a gem). It's her husband's lack of empathy and his unwillingness to prioritize his marriage over his mother. Anne feels all alone in her plight.

I cannot help but contrast Anne's situation (and that of so many women like her) to that of my friend who, upon turning to her parents for comfort during her first marital disagreement as a newlywed, received only three words from her father before he hung up the phone. "Leave and cleave," he told her. And another friend, longtime married now, still recalls the gift she most cherished from her wedding shower. Inside a beautifully wrapped box was an apron with the strings cut off. It was from her soon-to-be mother-in-law.

In marriages like Anne's, it's easy to pinpoint the frustration. What's hard to identify is the loneliness. But that's what results when the one meant to be her advocate is all too often her adversary. When a husband sits back and allows his wife to be selfishly manipulated, when he turns a blind eye as his wife gets her dreams, her plans, and her personality crushed, it's abandonment.

• • •

Worst of all, of course, is the loneliness of betrayal—the often irreversible loss of trust and the feelings of failure and inadequacy a wife experiences with a cheating husband. Added to that is the humiliation she feels when the adultery is made public. At least, when the betrayal is well known, a betrayed wife can find some comfort and support from friends who rally around her with love and outpourings of indignation on her behalf. For that reason, more private betrayals, while less humiliating perhaps, are the loneliest of all.

Such is the plight of Madeline, whose husband is a serial flirt. She dreads the endless weekend parties she feels obligated to attend with him, watching him out of the corner of her eye as he works the female guests, leaning in close with his charming intensity. Doesn't anyone else see it?

"That's just his personality," her friends tell her. "He doesn't mean anything by it."

"You're just paranoid," he tells her. But a wife knows.

She knows when he no longer finds her companionship sufficiently stimulating, when the grind of day-to-day married life has eroded romance into routine. She knows when his mind is elsewhere, even during their most intimate moments. She knows what others can't see, what her spouse won't confess. She is alone in her marriage.

• • •

The Christ-loving wife with an unbelieving husband is also no stranger to marital loneliness. She is unable to share the most important aspect of her life with the most important person in her life, and unless he comes to faith, there will be no remedy to this particular loneliness as long as they both shall live. Till death do us part. The home, the kids—everything that makes up a shared life—cannot span that particular chasm. Added to that is the constant friction of a sin-darkened heart rubbing against a Spirit-renewed one. "Do not be unequally yoked with unbelievers," Paul wrote. "For what partnership has righteousness with lawlessness? Or what fellowship has light with darkness?" (2 Cor. 6:14). A mismatched partnership such as this is no real partnership, and spiritual friction can, over time, lead to spiritual compromise.

Such are the difficulties of a Christian wife with an unbelieving husband, which, despite his single status, the pastor heart of Paul was well aware of. But he has encouragement to offer:

> If any woman has a husband who is an unbeliever, and he consents to live with her, she should not divorce him. For the unbelieving husband is made holy because of his wife, and the unbelieving wife is made holy because of her husband. . . . But if the unbelieving partner separates, let it be so. In such cases the brother or sister is not enslaved. God has called you to peace. For how do you know, wife, whether you will save your husband? (1 Cor. 7:13–16)

Paul takes that spiritual friction in another direction: as we live out our faith, in ways big and small, in both the major crises and the mundane happenings of day to day, we can be an influence. We can put the power of Christ and his cross on display, as Peter also writes:

Likewise, wives, be subject to your own husbands, so that even if some do not obey the word, they may be won without a word by the conduct of their wives, when they see your respectful and pure conduct. (1 Pet. 3:1–2)

The Realities of Marriage

The lonely wives we've glanced at are a small sampling to be sure, but sufficient to debunk the idea that marriage remedies loneliness. No doubt it remedies some kinds, but marriage has its own distinctive brand. Not for nothing did Paul write, "To the unmarried and the widows I say that it is good for them to remain single as I am. . . . Those who marry will have worldly troubles, and I would spare you that. . . . I want you to be free from anxieties" (1 Cor. 7:8, 28, 32). He had a realistic view of typical marital challenges:

The unmarried man is anxious about the things of the Lord, how to please the Lord. But the married man is anxious about worldly things, how to please his wife, and his interests are divided. And the unmarried or betrothed woman is anxious about the things of the Lord, how to be holy in body and spirit. But the married woman is anxious about worldly things, how to please her husband. I say this for your own benefit, not to lay any restraint upon you, but to promote good order and to secure your undivided devotion to the Lord. (1 Cor. 7:32–35)

If division of devotion is inherent in the marriage of two believers (and it is, according to Paul), then how much more of it characterizes the marriage of a believer to an unbeliever? Even when visible friction is absent, they are misaligned at the deepest heart level. No matter the makeup of a particular marriage, it will never be the loneliness remedy promised in fantasies and fairy tales.

Our Heavenly Husband

So what do we do with that depressingly big dose of reality? We turn our gaze to another reality that's even more life defining than marriage—to our heavenly husband, the Lord Jesus. If we belong to him, we belong to God's people, and together we make up the bride of Christ. Because that's true, this eternal marriage enables us to view our earthly one as God intended.

God gave marriage not as an end in itself but to point to that ultimate marriage, which will be so much better than even the best happily-ever-after marriage we read about in mass-market paperbacks. Marriage between a man and a woman is a temporary state, designed to serve as a symbol of the ultimate marriage that we will celebrate at the marriage supper of the Lamb, when Jesus comes back to take his bride home with him forever. Our temporary earthbound marriages are lonely because we marry sinners. And they are made more lonely when we look to them to be for us what they were never meant to be. Earthly marriage is part of the journey, not the destination. Our best marriage is yet to come, which is the consummation of all things and the joys that await us in the new heavens and the new earth.

"I'm looking forward to that," you might be saying, "but in the meantime, how do I survive the loneliness I'm facing in my here-and-now marriage?" That's a good question. So often—and rightly so—we are guided to derive our hope from what will happen at the end of time, when Jesus returns and we are finally in heaven, and while we believe it's true and we're grateful for it, it doesn't seem to help us very much with today. We do need to cultivate that long-range perspective. It's the one Scripture gives us, and it does so not because the hope of the future is meant to serve as some sort of emotional Xanax for the present but because we are eternal beings. The majority of our future lies in the next life. In fact, our time on earth is shorter than the blink of an eye in comparison. Our tangible *now* blinds us to the reality of our intangible eternity. Nevertheless, it's real. And keeping this reality in mind puts our marriage—and everything else about our life—in its right perspective.

Have you ever noticed that problems at home seem to diminish in scope when you go out of town for the week? It's not that the problems are less real; it's that you're taking in more of the world than you can grasp from home, and in the process, those back-at-home issues are diminished under a broader perspective. In Scripture we see the big picture, not just of our own life but also of God's purposes for the whole world. And there we see where it's all going. Everything now—the good and the bad—is leading to God's intended end. That's our destiny and our identity.

Yet Scripture also makes abundantly clear that those promised blessings have already begun for those in Christ, and we can participate in them even now through our union with Christ. Loneliness in marriage, whatever the cause, known or unknown, significantly diminishes as we come more fully to understand what our union with Christ entails. Although the marriage supper awaits a future day, our status as bride has been settled. We are even now engaged to Christ. Marriage on earth is a temporary, sin-tainted shadow of our forever marriage, and the husband we have now is meant to point us to the One we will have forever. That's why Paul issued these instructions to husbands:

> Husbands, love your wives, as Christ loved the church and
> gave himself up for her, that he might sanctify her, having

cleansed her by the washing of water with the word, so that he might present the church to himself in splendor, without spot or wrinkle or any such thing, that she might be holy and without blemish. In the same way husbands should love their wives as their own bodies. He who loves his wife loves himself. For no one ever hated his own flesh, but nourishes and cherishes it, just as Christ does the church, because we are members of his body. "Therefore a man shall leave his father and mother and hold fast to his wife, and the two shall become one flesh." This mystery is profound, and I am saying that it refers to Christ and the church. (Eph. 5:25–32)

Do you see it? Marriage now, on earth, is a symbol for marriage later, in heaven. And because it's a symbol, it will never measure up to the real thing. Our husband will never offer us perfectly sacrificial love, or be constantly zealous for our growth, or cherish us thoroughly. He cannot be Christ for us. He is a sinner, as are we. To view him as a surrogate savior is to intensify our loneliness.

A Wife's Fulfillment

Did we really think marriage was the answer to life? It's a tremendous blessing, for sure, and has been God's design for most people since the time of creation. One of the primary reasons God instituted marriage was to provide us with the blessings of companionship (Gen. 2:18), yet it was never his intention to displace himself from man's heart in the process. Too often we look to our marriage to define us, making of it something it was never meant to be. When we do that, our sense of well-being rides the roller coaster of our marriage, feeling up when it's good and down when it's not. The way to get off that ride is found only in recognizing that our union with Christ—now, today—is deeper and more defining than even our marital union.

So rather than asking God to make our marriage more fulfilling, let's ask him to work through it to show us more of Christ. As we lean into our heavenly Bridegroom, we will find what no earthly husband can ever give us.

• • •

Questions for Discussion or Reflection from Chapter 11

1. If you are married, what aspects of marriage are different from what you expected? If you are single, how do the illustrations in chapter 11 alter your view of marriage?

2. What is distinctive about the loneliness in a spiritually mismatched marriage? See 2 Corinthians 6:14–18. What hope does the New Testament provide to lonely wives in such a marriage?

3. How do the realities of married life shown in 1 Corinthians 7 adjust our marital expectations? In turn, how might adjusting our expectations alleviate some of our loneliness?

4. Discuss from Scripture why God gave marriage. See especially Ephesians 5:25–33.

5. How can our marital loneliness serve as an avenue to better grasp all we have in our union with Christ? Name some specific ways.

The world's fierce winds are blowing,
temptation sharp and keen.
I have a peace in knowing
my Savior stands between—
He stands to shield me from danger
when my friends are all gone.
He promised never to leave me,
never to leave me alone! . . .

When in affliction's valley
I tread the road of care,
My Savior helps me carry
the cross so heavy to bear;
Though all around me is darkness,
earthly joys all flown;
My Savior whispers His promise,
never to leave me alone! . . .

—Ludie D. Pickett, "Never Alone"

12

The Loneliness of
Being Unmarried

When I step up to a podium to speak on the topic of singleness (a relatively common occurrence, given that I am single), I scan the audience for a certain type of young woman. She is the one slunk down in her seat, face lowered and arms crossed tightly across her body. She has come only because someone urged her to attend; now that she's here, everything in her wants to run for the door so she won't have to hear yet another talk on this topic. Her body language conveys a bit of hostility and a lot of fear. She has heard it all before from older women, some married, some single. She dreads the single speakers most of all, and that's because she's afraid that the fearful malady—middle-aged spinsterhood—might be contagious. There's at least one in every crowd, and for that reason I am sure to point out as I begin one of these talks that we single women of a certain age are the exception; God's normative design is marriage.

Why So Much Singleness?

Since marriage is God's normal ordering, why does God allow so many of us to remain single? There are about as many single adults in America today as married ones. One reason is that women's lives have significantly changed over the past few generations. Just a few decades ago, most women upon completing their education expected to settle down and raise a family. Today, women get the same degrees and hold the same jobs as men, which has led to female independence like no other time in history. No one can argue that good has come from the society-wide recognition that men and women have equal value. But the changes haven't all been positive.

The impact on marriage is one of those negatives. As women's opportunities have increased, so have their expectations. Lots of women are unwilling to marry a man who has less education than she does, or one who makes less money, so she chooses not to marry at all. The same is true in reverse: many men don't get overly excited at the prospect of marrying a woman who is more educated or better paid. Decades ago, a woman didn't seek to build an impressive resume as a way to build security— she found a husband. Altogether, the contemporary blurring of gender roles has diminished men's opportunities to be masculine and has taken from women a female vulnerability that used to be prized. This, among other things, has contributed to the overall decline of marriage today, and Christians are not exempt, although it ought not to be that way. In the Old Testament, God forbade the prophet Jeremiah from marrying, as a way to warn people of coming judgment due to sin (Jer. 16:1–4), but believers today have an opportunity to demonstrate the exact opposite:

> God's commands for Jeremiah are not his commands for the Christian church. The gospel age is a time for matrimony,

a time for sympathy, and a time for revelry. . . . The gospel age is a good time to get married. Jeremiah 33 promises that in the streets of Jerusalem "There shall be heard again the voice of mirth and the voice of gladness, the voice of the bridegroom and the voice of the bride" (vv. 10, 11). This promise has come true in Jesus Christ. It is no accident that the first miracle Jesus performed was to turn water into wine at a wedding (John 2:1–11). When the Savior comes, it is time for wedding and for song.[13]

God delights in marriage; our culture overall no longer does—at least, not marriage as defined by God. This along with the shift in gender roles explains the prevalence of singleness.

God Determines Our Marital Destiny

So where does that leave us? Are we doomed to a life of solitary aloneness because we live in a morally bankrupt society or because women's-rights fights send would-be spouses running for the hills? Indeed we might remain single—let's face that possibility head-on. That being said, society is most definitely not the determiner of our marital status—yours or mine. Only God is. He decides who marries and who doesn't. Forget the statistics; they are a waste of time for those who know the character of God. If marriage is God's plan for us, sooner or later, we're going to get married. Either way, we can be sure that solitary aloneness is not his plan. He has called us to live in community, in a family of believers, and he undertakes to get us there. "God settles the solitary in a home," the psalmist tells us (Ps. 68:6). The real question, therefore, isn't whether we will wind up alone; it's whether we're willing for the provision of companionship to be something other than marriage.

So dealing with lonely singleness begins with our heart. Do

we trust God? We won't trust him if we don't believe he is good, and I don't mean "good" in just a general sort of way. I mean "good" concerning how he governs the details of our individual lives—including our marital status. Singleness for today is God's being good to us today. Do you believe that? If so, that's real trust, and it won't get snuffed out under those bouts of longing that plague us all from time to time and the loneliness that often triggers them.

Single and Lonely

Just as there is loneliness unique to marriage, there is a loneliness particular to singleness. It's what a young single woman feels when her friends get engaged and begin planning their weddings, while she has no prospect on the horizon. It's what the thirty-something single feels when her married friends give birth while her own body clock is beginning to wind down. It's what the forty-year-old feels when others refer to her marriage potential in the past tense: "You remind me of my Great-Aunt Betty. She never married either."

Unmarried loneliness is fueled by such comments, as well as by the marital happiness we perceive (or imagine) others are enjoying. However, trusting God when those remarks are made isn't about pasting on a passive smile and simply praying for greater patience. It's about leaning more deeply into Christ and finding in the process all the blessings of our union with him—a deeper, more joy-filled union than even that of marriage. As we rest in Christ and trust in the goodness of our heavenly Father, the loneliness of being single becomes an opportunity to build up the whole body of Christ. *We can serve our believing community and glorify God not despite our singleness but by virtue of it.*

No Pity, Please

First, as the fruit of our abiding becomes evident, both to ourselves and to the people around us, we demonstrate that singles aren't to be pitied. The fruit of our faith will be evidenced in the way we talk about our singleness. We'll find that we can be appropriately honest about our difficulties and our longings in such a way as to convey that as much as we'd love to be married, that dream isn't the substance of our hope. We practice what we're told in God's Word: "Let us hold fast the confession of our hope without wavering, for he who promised is faithful. And let us consider how to stir up one another to love and good works" (Heb. 10:23–24). Married or single, friendships in the church are meant to include confessions of hope that are based on the truth of God's faithfulness, and as we engage in that kind of conversation, we motivate one another to be others-focused and God-centered.

Married people often do feel sorry for singles, and sometimes the discomfort that accompanies those feelings can lead them to shy away from us altogether. We, the single ones, can work toward unity by how we talk about it—and by how we receive what is said. A pastor friend, who has been happily married since his early twenties, once said to me, "I don't know how you stand it. I can't imagine being single." He wasn't offering pity— he was opening up about himself. And far from this leading me to self-pity, it had the opposite effect. I felt validated because his honesty pointed to both the hardships of singleness and the grace God has provided me for it.

Singleness Is Not a Problem to Be Solved

Second, as we abide in Christ, we will stop viewing singleness as a problem to be solved. I've heard many an intercessory prayer

that lumps singles together with the sick and the dying—a cat-
egorical mistake when considered from a biblical perspective:

> Singleness lived to the glory of God and the furtherance of
> his kingdom testifies to the complete sufficiency of Christ for
> all things. The Christian is fully blessed in Christ, whether he
> or she is married or single, rich or poor, in comfort or duress.
> The distinctive calling of singleness within the church testi-
> fies to this truth. . . . Within the church this message is also in
> need of fresh articulation. Our youth are subject to an end-
> less barrage of confusing messages concerning relationships
> and sexuality. Our culture idolizes the never-satiated lusts
> for sexual intimacy and the trappings of material comforts.
> To this end the Christian church needs to be intentional in
> teaching the biblical vision for both Christian singleness and
> Christian marriage. This entails not "Christianizing" the
> pervasive relational and material lusts of our culture into a
> preoccupation with building perfect families and exquisite
> homes. What is needed is a vision for promoting lifestyles
> in accordance with the fundamental tenets of the gospel,
> that the kingdom of God is at hand and that consummate
> satisfaction is to be found ultimately only in being reconciled
> to our God in Jesus Christ.[14]

Since there will be no marriage in heaven, singles have an
opportunity to showcase to both the church and the surround-
ing world a foretaste of what heaven will be like. Can you see
how singleness can be put forth as a sign of hope rather than of
despair? We can project this hope to our married brothers and
sisters by how we handle our singleness, and we can also display
the love of Christ to other singles who feel shut out from the
best life has to offer.

The fact that "God sets the solitary in a home" (Ps. 68:6) tells us something about God's character—he delights in family, which is what "home" implies, and he delights to bring all his people into one. In keeping with God's Word, Christians place a high value on family, but in the new-covenant era—our era—the family that Scripture emphasizes most of all is the church family, not the nuclear family. When that priority gets reversed, it hinders rather than helps the building up of the church overall.

Given the society-wide breakdown of the family, we can certainly understand why churches want to stress its importance, but many bend too far in that other direction to the point where family—father, mother, and three kids—is idolized. If we consider what the apostles emphasized, we see that their focus was much more on the Great Commission, personal holiness, and growing the church family. And it is this family from which no single Christian is to be left out.

No doubt sin and selfishness have contributed to the prevalence of singleness today. There are men who don't want to grow up and take on the responsibility of leading a family, and there are women who hold out for a rich, successful man while bypassing a godly one. But to allow that sad reality to cast singleness in a negative light is to forget the words of Paul, who said: "To the unmarried and the widows I say that it is good for them to remain single as I am" (1 Cor. 7:8). And it is to forget the words of Jesus, who said, "There are eunuchs who have been so from birth, and there are eunuchs who have been made eunuchs by men, and there are eunuchs who have made themselves eunuchs for the sake of the kingdom of heaven. Let the one who is able to receive this receive it" (Matt. 19:12).

Eunuchs were men unable to experience sexual arousal for one reason or another, and that's why Jesus mentions them here in Matthew 19, in a discussion with his disciples about marriage—the only biblically legitimate context for sexual activity—and singleness. As we consider the implications of his words, we see that some people are single due to circumstances beyond their control, and others choose it. The bottom line is, when it comes to singleness and marriage, the New Testament shows us that neither is wrong and both are good.

Unique Opportunities

Third, as we abide in Christ, discovering the riches of being united to him, we discover, often much to our surprise, the unique blessings that come with being single. At a purely practical level, we have more control over our time than our married counterparts ("more control over" is key there, countering the common but mistaken view that singles have more time in general).

Singles have more discretion over the use of money as well. As a single woman, I can pick up a rotisserie chicken for dinner and, before sitting down to eat, read my Bible for an hour. Most of my married friends are focused on preparing a family meal at that hour, one that rarely includes a precooked chicken (too small to feed a family, but four meals for a single woman). The unmarried can more readily live out their personal preferences not only when it comes to meals but also in planning weekend activities, vacations, and areas of service in the church and community.

A while back I read a blog post by a married Christian in which she criticized single women as selfish for enjoying such blessings. Can you imagine a Christian writing a similar article for married women, rebuking them for enjoying the blessings unique to marriage? I thought not. We singles encourage one another and bring glory to God when we identify our unique blessings, embrace them, and put them to good use. "Do not be deceived, my beloved brothers. Every good gift and every perfect gift is from above, coming down from the Father of lights with whom there is no variation or shadow due to change" (James 1:16–17).

The best privilege of being single is far and away the increased opportunity for discipleship and serving our Savior. This more than anything else—including marriage—addresses our loneliness. Like Mary, we have more opportunity to sit at Jesus's feet and learn (Luke 10:38–42). Like Mary Magdalene, we have greater exposure to the wonders of the resurrection (John 20:11–18). Like Anna, we have more mobility to get out and share the gospel (Luke 2:38). Like Lydia, we have more flexibility to use our homes and resources to serve the church (Acts 16:15, 40).

There is a certain fulfillment that comes from living out these unique advantages that our married brothers and sisters can't fully know, and as we embrace these opportunities with gratitude, we demonstrate to our entire faith community the value and rewards of remaining unmarried.

Blessing Because Of, Not in Spite Of

We want that, don't we? We want to know—not on paper but in our heart and in the places we live out our faith—that we have value, not despite our singleness but actually *because* of it. When a woman has never been pursued by a man, or if she has been rejected by one (or more), she so easily questions her personal worth. It is to such women that Christ comes, not to shore up their self-esteem but to drive them to find *him* as their worth. It is in valuing Christ that our own value becomes clear, and as that happens, we discover that we have ceased to define ourselves by our marital status. We don't need to be Mrs. So-

and-So to have a respectable identity. Spiritually speaking, we're already a "Mrs." in Christ. Our whole identity is bound up with the person of Christ, and that's true for every believer, married or single. All this speaks deeply and directly to aspects of loneliness that we're aware of at some level but can't quite put our finger on. As we fellowship with our Savior and find our identity in him rather than in our marital status, we can participate more fully in our faith community because we no longer feel so self-consciously single.

Being Single to the Glory of God

We can also help others within our fellowship along these same lines, especially if the church we attend tends to divide church members demographically. You know what I mean: there's the singles' group (or two—one for young adults and another for the over-forty set); the small group for young married couples; the monthly luncheon for seniors; and the various youth groups broken out by age. We certainly don't want to negate the positive benefits of these demographically based subgroups, yet we want to be aware that too much emphasis on demographics hides the spiritual reality that everyone in that church body is part of one family. We don't want to lose sight of what Paul said: "As it is, there are many parts, yet one body. The eye cannot say to the hand, 'I have no need of you,' nor again the head to the feet, 'I have no need of you'" (1 Cor. 12:20–21). Married church members benefit from single members, and singles benefit from the married men and women in their midst. That's how Christ intends his church to thrive.

Certainly church singles' groups are a blessing; they provide an ideal means for marriages to form, and lifelong friendships often begin here. Singles' groups can be detrimental to spiritual health, however, when they become their own little church within a church or when they take the place of Sunday worship. A church's singles' ministry can—and should—serve as an entry point into the larger church body, but if it becomes an end in itself, no one benefits ultimately, including the singles themselves. Those in their late forties who linger in the singles' group they began attending in their early twenties, while never entering into the larger church body, become over time a sort of sad singles' support group. Can you see the law of diminishing returns at work there? It doesn't abate our loneliness; it entrenches us more deeply in it. The hand needs the foot, and the eye needs the ear. So, in the strength Christ provides (Phil. 4:19), it is good to leave the protective cocoon of the safe and familiar—the easy and comfortable—and involve ourselves in the lives of others to whom God will surely send us.

If that fails to wow you, it might be because, when you think of involving yourself more fully in the church, what comes to mind are particular ministries toward which singles tend to gravitate or toward which the church tends to push them—children's programs, for example, or working in the nursery so as to give moms a much-needed break. Of course, getting involved with the children in our church not only proves helpful to tired moms; it can also serve as balm for the single woman with an aching maternal heart. But that's not true for all single women. Some of us are simply not gifted to work with children, and, guess what? That's okay. Having a preference for areas of service besides child care doesn't make us less feminine or useful to the body of Christ. The need isn't always the call, and opportunity isn't always the answer, and we can be lovingly candid when this is the case for us. Truthfulness, if expressed in love, breeds unifying fellowship.

Married or unmarried, we all have particular gifts, and we serve the body best, and find the most joy in serving, when we uncover them and put them to use. If God hasn't called us to raise a family or gifted us to work with children, we can be sure he has called us to something else, and as we dedicate ourselves to serving our faith community, God delights to show us the unique ways he has gifted us for the furthering of our joy, the good of the church, and his own glory.

In God's economy, singleness isn't second best. To the contrary, it's a privileged calling with unique blessings to enjoy and to pour out for others. Are we willing for that unless, or until, God calls us to marriage? Tell him of your willingness, and, if you're not quite there yet, ask him to lead you to it. You have nothing to lose but loneliness.

A Life Worth Living

"Nothing to lose but loneliness"—those words aren't just a trite wrap-up to a chapter on being single and lonely. Those words are true. I know it, because I've lived it. Earlier in my life, singleness was just a synonym for disappointment (not to mention frustration with an occasional dose of bitterness). During that season, I poured my life into trying to change my marital status, but, as is true whenever we embark on ventures without God, it led only to more disappointment. But one night, God in his grace brought me to the end of myself. I remember every detail about that night, how I was sitting alone in my dark apartment, facing the end of what had been a promising relationship. I prayed, "God, if marriage isn't the plan for now, what is? You know what I've wanted, but now I'm asking, what do *you* want to do with my life?"

Surprisingly, the depressing resignation with which I'd started the prayer was gone when I finished, and in its place was a sense of hopeful expectation. Trust. I'd prayed all this before, but there was something different this time—I really meant it. Only God could have gotten me to that place. And he did.

Afterward, within a very short time, new opportunities came knocking—work that has given me fulfillment and real contentment ever since. Of course there are still hours and days of loneliness, but as of that night long ago, loneliness ceased being the dominant theme of my life. The work I do is really only a small part of why; it's that during that nighttime prayer, my heart opened much more fully to the lordship of Christ. The blessing I find in my work and the contentment I know both spring directly from that.

I was helped back then by a godly woman who had walked the path of singleness for decades. I observed how she lived, pouring out her life for Christ in service to the church we were both a part of. She had very little in the way of material assets, but she seemed not to notice or care. I don't know how she felt about being single, because she never talked about herself. Somehow, conversations *with* her were never *about* her.

A few years ago, she reached retirement age and made plans to step down from her role in the church as she entered this new season. When I heard the news, I thanked God for weaving her into my life all those years earlier, an example of joyful singleness lived out decade after decade to the glory of God. So you can imagine my surprise when I found out that she was engaged to be married. An elderly widower had come into her life and swept her off her feet. She was the most radiant bride I have ever seen, and the radiance didn't fade when the wedding was over. Her groom adored her and lavished on her affection as well as material blessings she'd never imagined.

So there you have my story. And you have the story of my friend. Both reveal that God delights to bless those who put their trust in him. Both reveal that he is not insensitive to the stigma of being alone and the loneliness that accompanies it. I am still making my way down this path—I certainly haven't arrived yet. But single or married, I want to live life like my friend before me, who found the words of an unmarried prophet to be true:

> The steadfast love of the LORD never ceases;
>> his mercies never come to an end;
> they are new every morning;
>> great is your faithfulness.
> "The LORD is my portion," says my soul,
>> "therefore I will hope in him." (Lam. 3:22–24)

Don't you?

• • •

Questions for Discussion or Reflection from Chapter 12

1. Discuss the various reasons singleness is so prevalent today. How does the character of God factor in to what we see?

2. What are the implications of Psalm 68:6?

3. Discuss the statement from page 136: "We can serve our believing community and glorify God not despite our singleness but by virtue of it."

4. What aspect of our union with Christ alters our view of our marital status?

5. Discuss some of the unique blessings of being single.

Part 3

LONELINESS
REDEEMED

The church's one foundation is Jesus Christ, her Lord;
she is his new creation by water and the Word.
From heaven he came and sought her to be his holy bride;
with his own blood he bought her, and for her life he died.

Elect from every nation, yet one o'er all the earth;
her charter of salvation: one Lord, one faith, one birth.
One holy name she blesses, partakes one holy food,
and to one hope she presses, with every grace endued.

Though with a scornful wonder the world see her
       oppressed,
by schisms rent asunder, by heresies distressed,
yet saints their watch are keeping; their cry goes up:
       "How long?"
and soon the night of weeping shall be the morn of song.

Mid toil and tribulation, and tumult of her war,
she waits the consummation of peace forevermore,
till with the vision glorious her longing eyes are blest,
and the great church victorious shall be the church at rest.

Yet she on earth hath union with God the Three in One,
and mystic sweet communion with those whose rest
       is won:
O happy ones and holy! Lord, give us grace that we
like them, the meek and lowly, may live eternally.

      —Samuel J. Stone, "The Church's One Foundation"

13

In the Family of God's People

"The church as an institution is so outdated," some claim today. "We need to stop going to church and start *being* the church." Have you heard that lately? It's trendy. And it's coming from the mouths of the disillusioned, those who have witnessed one leadership scandal too many. It comes also from those who either don't know or are seeking to avoid clear biblical revelation. An increasing number desire to redefine Jesus by today's cultural standards so they can feel comfortable and avoid facing the reality of sin.

When the Church Stops Being the Church

Sadly, there have been numerous high-profile scandals in recent years, bringing dishonor to Christ and damaging the reputation of the church overall. Even more prevalent, however, is the destructive impact wrought by churches that stray from Scripture in an attempt to make Jesus more relevant for today.

There we find a Jesus whose love would never condemn

the lifestyle of one's choosing. Those who promote this kind of Jesus wish to make the church a safe place for the lonely and marginalized, but in the process they wind up fostering the very problem they wish to solve. One popular author recently wrote:

> It is high time Christians opened wide their arms, wide their churches, wide their tables, wide their homes to the LGBT community. . . . Here are my arms open wide. So wide that every last one of you can jump inside. You are so dear, so beloved, so precious and important. You matter so desperately and your life is worthy and beautiful. There is nothing "wrong with you," or in any case, nothing more right or wrong than any of us, which is to say we are all hopelessly screwed up but Jesus still loves us beyond all reason and lives to make us all new, restored, whole. Yay for Jesus![15]

The author is absolutely right about the need to share the love of Christ with the lost, regardless of the sin that characterizes them. But she goes biblically astray—and directs the lost straight toward hell—when she tells them, "There is nothing 'wrong with you.'" Such thinking actually obscures the real Jesus—the one whom the marginalized so desperately need:

> It's tiring (not to mention saddening) to watch Christian leaders tell individuals that you're born who you are, how you are, and that's okay. Nothing is wrong with you. Essentially saying, everyone is born inherently good. But that's a dangerously deceptive attitude. What good then is the Good News if everyone is born good and hunky-dory? What's the point of Jesus' suffering and dying on the cross? Christ died not only because of how much he loves us, but also to pay the price of our sin and conquer our broken humanity.[16]

Churches that proclaim inclusion without repentance—a growing number—are not proclaiming the true gospel; therefore, they are not true churches. The only true ones are those modeled upon the New Testament, and it is in such churches that the lonely and marginalized find forgiveness, cleansing from sin, and the belonging for which they yearn.

They will not find those things in entertainment-based settings that seek to set forth a warm, fuzzy, culturally relevant Jesus. When self-empowerment and human feel-good are the top priorities, the true gospel and the glory of God are not. As someone wisely said about efforts to woo the lost, what you win them with is what you win them to. To reinvent church into a so-called safe space or judgment-free zone does not win anything of eternal value for anyone.

I recall once asking one of these relevance pastors, "Do you believe that the Word and the Spirit are sufficient to change lives?"

"To a point," he replied.

How sad. The Lord of the universe needs no help or hoopla from man. He is mighty to save. That's why all this so-called attractional stuff really doesn't matter, and it is not what the lost need. And the lonely who wander into such churches looking for the "home" God holds out in Psalm 68:6 will leave disillusioned. The lost and the lonely need Jesus—the real one—and they need churches that proclaim him as he is shown in Scripture. A real church as set forth in the New Testament is not a support group. It's not a social club or a counseling center. It's a family of redeemed sinners who have God as their Father through their union with Jesus Christ. It's a body knit together by the Holy Spirit so that together all are built up and strengthened and loved. Church is God's idea. It is his protection and provision for his people. Spiritually speaking, we do not grow well in isolation. God planned that we grow in fellowship with other believers, sinners rubbing up against sinners, giving and receiving the love of Christ. In this lifetime, the church is where loneliness is redeemed.

Vitally Connected

The church is also where we are meant to use our personal gifts and talents. When we are united to Christ by faith, we are empowered by the Spirit with special gifts. These gifts are assigned to us individually, but each one is given for the benefit of all. In other words, our spiritual gifts have a specific God-given purpose:

> Now there are varieties of gifts, but the same Spirit; and there are varieties of service, but the same Lord; and there are varieties of activities, but it is the same God who empowers them all in everyone. To each is given the manifestation of the Spirit *for the common good*. (1 Cor. 12:4–7)

Are you beginning to see why the church as God intended it is where our loneliness can be redeemed? We don't have to be ashamed of that deep yearning in our heart to connect with people—God designed us to want that:

> God arranged the members in the body, each one of them, as he chose. If all were a single member, where would the body be? As it is, there are many parts, yet one body. The eye cannot say to the hand, "I have no need of you," nor again the head to the feet, "I have no need of you." (1 Cor. 12:18–21)

Whatever our particular gift—high-profile or behind the scenes—it matters. It counts. And if we don't put it to use in the local church to which God has called us, everyone in that church is the poorer for it.

Comforted Together

By God's design, we belong to one another. For that reason, not only our gifts but also our joys and our sufferings are meant to be lived out in fellowship with other believers. "If one member suffers, all suffer together; if one member is honored, all rejoice together," Paul said (1 Cor. 12:26). God promises to comfort us when suffering comes, and a primary way he does this is through the love and support of those in our faith community. This in turn equips us to turn around and help others going through similar trials:

> Blessed be the God and Father of our Lord Jesus Christ, the Father of mercies and God of all comfort, who comforts us in all our affliction, so that we may be able to comfort those who are in any affliction, with the comfort with which we ourselves are comforted by God. For as we share abundantly in Christ's sufferings, so through Christ we share abundantly in comfort too. (2 Cor. 1:3–5)

God intends for us to experience his comfort primarily in the fellowship of other believers.

Intimacy with Christ

It might sound counterintuitive, but according to what Jesus prayed—first for his disciples and then for us too—we as individuals will know our oneness with him most fully when we do life together with other believers:

> I do not ask for these only, but also for those who will believe in me through their word, that they may all be one, just

> as you, Father, are in me, and I in you, that they also may be
> in us, so that the world may believe that you have sent me.
> (John 17:20–21)

And according to Paul, we will know the protective love of
Christ most fully not on our own but as part of the church:

> For no one ever hated his own flesh, but nourishes and cher-
> ishes it, just as Christ does the church, because we are mem-
> bers of his body. (Eph. 5:29–30)

Church is also the context in which we come to know the
character of our God—Father, Son, and Holy Spirit. Of course
we grow in our understanding of God as we read his Word in
our solitary hours, but God has specially equipped some with
the ability and the calling to teach it to the rest of us. It's so
easy to get rooted in wrong thinking about God when we rely
solely on our private devotions, which is why we need to place
ourselves under those whom God has raised up for that purpose.
"No prophecy of Scripture comes from someone's own interpre-
tation," Peter wrote (2 Pet. 1:20).

Priorities, Priorities . . .

That's just a small sampling of all we see in Scripture about the
necessity of church involvement. Participation in a local church
is God's will for us. Let me say that again: *participation in a
local church is God's will for us.* It is there that we are meant to
serve and be served by others. It's the primary way we grow up
in our faith. If we've been keeping our local fellowship at arm's
length, perhaps our recent bouts with loneliness are a Spirit-
prompted nudge to get us back there. Excuses for staying away
are always easy to find: new music, old music, too early, too late,
preaching style, praying format, not enough of this, too much

of that. Of course there are valid reasons to leave a church, but the call away from a particular fellowship is definitely not the call away from church altogether:

> Let us consider how to stir up one another to love and good works, *not neglecting to meet together*, as is the habit of some, but encouraging one another, and all the more as you see the Day drawing near. (Heb. 10:24–25)

Involvement in a particular church in a particular place is a top priority, biblically speaking. If we place it low on our personal priority list, we're going to miss out on the blessings of this divinely appointed provision for our loneliness. If the choices we've made for a house or a job or something else have isolated us from a biblically sound church, then it's worth changing our life to get it back. If we do, we are sure to find what Jesus promised:

> Truly, I say to you, there is no one who has left house or brothers or sisters or mother or father or children or lands, for my sake and for the gospel, who will not receive a hundredfold now in this time, houses and brothers and sisters and mothers and children and lands, with persecutions, and in the age to come eternal life. (Mark 10:29–30)

• • •

Questions for Discussion or Reflection from Chapter 13

1. What is your view of church, and what has shaped your view?

2. Based on the passages covered in chapter 13, why is church involvement a necessity for believers?

3. Review 1 Corinthians 12:1–31. In what particular ways have you been gifted to participate in building up the body of

Christ? How are you using your gifts? Discuss the impact your service has had on your loneliness.

4. What characteristics are necessary for a church to be considered biblically sound? Form your answer from specific New Testament passages.

5. Is lack of church involvement a primary factor in your loneliness? If so, what will you do to change that? When will you make these changes, and who will hold you accountable?

Ah, holy Jesus, how hast Thou offended,
That man to judge Thee hath in hate pretended?
By foes derided, by Thine own rejected,
O most afflicted.

Who was the guilty? Who brought this upon Thee?
Alas, my treason, Jesus, hath undone Thee.
'Twas I, Lord, Jesus, I it was denied Thee!
I crucified Thee.

Lo, the Good Shepherd for the sheep is offered;
The slave hath sinned, and the Son hath suffered;
For man's atonement, while he nothing heedeth,
God intercedeth.

For me, kind Jesus, was Thy incarnation,
Thy mortal sorrow, and Thy life's oblation;
Thy death of anguish and Thy bitter passion,
For my salvation.

Therefore, kind Jesus, since I cannot pay Thee,
I do adore Thee, and will ever pray Thee,
Think on Thy pity and Thy love unswerving,
Not my deserving.

—Johann Heerman,
"Ah, Holy Jesus, How Hast Thou Offended"

Conclusion

The Man of Sorrows

Young or old, single or married, male or female—no one escapes loneliness, at least, not in this lifetime. But the reality of our loneliness isn't all bleak. In fact, as we've seen in the previous thirteen chapters, it's actually an opportunity and a sign of hope. Our loneliness points to the fact that something is missing. If we were to get everything we ever wanted here and now, if all our circumstances were to fall into place the way we wish, the truth is we would still be lonely. Ultimately, our less than perfect circumstances aren't the reason we are lonely; our circumstances simply bring out the loneliness that's already there. It's there because right now, in this life, we aren't home yet. Loneliness won't be eradicated until we are finally at home in heaven, completely free from the presence of sin—both ours and that of others—and in the presence of the Lord. God created us in such a way that we are complete only in and with him, which is why it's not until we have been perfected in glory that will we be forever free from the feeling that something is missing—that thing we call "loneliness."

The Answer to Everything

Although that fulfillment awaits a future day, the eradication of our loneliness begins the moment we come to Christ, because we are united to him. We are *in* him. Do you know what it means to be "in Christ"? The New Testament is filled to the brim with all it means, and all of it speaks directly into our loneliness.

Sin makes us lonely, but in Christ the penalty and power of sin are broken, and its presence is already beginning to fade:

> There is therefore now no condemnation for those who are in Christ Jesus. For the law of the Spirit of life has set you free in Christ Jesus from the law of sin and death. (Rom. 8:1–2)

Being unloved makes us lonely, but in Christ we are fully loved:

> Who shall separate us from the love of Christ? Shall tribulation, or distress, or persecution, or famine, or nakedness, or danger, or sword? . . . No, in all these things we are more than conquerors through him who loved us. For I am sure that neither death nor life, nor angels nor rulers, nor things present nor things to come, nor powers, nor height nor depth, nor anything else in all creation, will be able to separate us from the love of God in Christ Jesus our Lord. (Rom. 8:35–39)

The bad decisions we make isolate us from others and intensify loneliness, but in Christ we have wisdom:

> God chose what is foolish in the world to shame the wise; God chose what is weak in the world to shame the strong; God chose what is low and despised in the world, even things that are not, to bring to nothing things that are, so that no human being might boast in the presence of God.

And because of him you are in Christ Jesus, who became to us wisdom from God, righteousness and sanctification and redemption. (1 Cor. 1:27–30)

Suffering breaks our heart, but in Christ the loneliness of heartbreak is transformed:

Blessed be the God and Father of our Lord Jesus Christ, the Father of mercies and God of all comfort, who comforts us in all our affliction, so that we may be able to comfort those who are in any affliction, with the comfort with which we ourselves are comforted by God. For as we share abundantly in Christ's sufferings, so through Christ we share abundantly in comfort too. (2 Cor. 1:3–5)

Our regrettable past can entrench us in the loneliness of shame, all too easily defining both our present and our future, but in Christ the past loses its hold over us:

Therefore, if anyone is in Christ, he is a new creation. The old has passed away; behold, the new has come. (2 Cor. 5:17)

Abandonment by a parent or someone else we love devastates us with loneliness, but in Christ, God has become our Father, and he will never leave us:

In Christ Jesus you are all sons of God, through faith. (Gal. 3:26)

Being left off the guest list brings on the loneliness of being unwanted, but God chose us to belong to him:

Blessed be the God and Father of our Lord Jesus Christ, who has blessed us in Christ with every spiritual blessing in the heavenly places, even as he chose us in him before the foundation of the world, that we should be holy and blameless before him. In love he predestined us for adoption to himself as sons through Jesus Christ, according to the purpose of his will, to the praise of his glorious grace, with which he has blessed us in the Beloved. (Eph. 1:3–6)

When our labors are unappreciated, we feel the loneliness of not mattering, but in Christ our service has eternal value:

For we are his workmanship, created in Christ Jesus for good works, which God prepared beforehand, that we should walk in them. (Eph. 2:10)

Even when we are isolated from friends, family, or people in general, we are never really alone:

But now in Christ Jesus you who once were far off have been brought near by the blood of Christ. (Eph. 2:13)

Jesus Understands Because He's Been There

We could go on forever about all the blessings of being in Christ. The point here is to show how our union with him is the beginning of the end of our loneliness. Jesus delights to meet us in our lonely places and give us himself. After all, he understands what it means to be lonely:

He was despised and rejected by men,
      a man of sorrows and acquainted with grief;
and as one from whom men hide their faces
      he was despised, and we esteemed him not. (Isa. 53:3)

People hated him while he walked this earth, and people still hate him today. Yet he continues to hold out love to his haters. He chose loneliness in order to relieve ours. Jesus took on all our loneliness at the cross, where he was left alone to die, cut off even from his beloved Father. He knows the agony of loneliness, of being utterly alone, which we hear in his cry from the cross: "My God, my God, why have you forsaken me?" (Matt. 27:46). Because he was forsaken, we are not. People may reject us, but we will never be forsaken by the one who matters most—God himself.

Unlike Jesus, we bring a good bit of our loneliness on ourselves through sin and selfishness. Unlike Jesus, we deserve to be lonely. Being left alone is a fit consequence for sin. But Christ hasn't left us there. He has come to rescue us from ourselves and all we do to destroy our lives and our relationships. He gives us himself when the people we love have left us. And he fills up from himself what no person or circumstance in this life can ever fill—that aching place in our heart we call "loneliness." During his earthly life and in his death on the cross, Jesus *did* loneliness for us. He is back with his Father now, and he comes to take us there too. Close your reading of this book with Jesus's words to lonely hearts:

> Let not your hearts be troubled. Believe in God; believe also in me. In my Father's house are many rooms. If it were not so, would I have told you that I go to prepare a place for you? And if I go and prepare a place for you, I will come again and will take you to myself, that where I am you may be also. . . . I am the way, and the truth, and the life. (John 14:1–3, 6)

Notes

1. Christopher West, cited in Gary Barnes and Darrell L. Bock, "5 Myths and Truths in Loneliness" (August 21, 2015), accessed August 24, 2015, http://www.thegospelcoalition.org/article/5-myths-and-truths-in -loneliness.
2. Barry Cooper, "The Problem of Your Choices," *Desiring God* website (February 5, 2015), accessed August 27, 2015, http://www.desiringgod .org/articles/the-problem-of-your-choices.
3. David Powlison, "Dynamics of Biblical Change," class notes, Christian Counseling and Educational Foundation (CCEF), 2002.
4. Barnes and Bock, "5 Myths and Truths in Loneliness."
5. Ibid.
6. Elisabeth Elliot, *The Path of Loneliness: Finding Your Way through the Wilderness to God* (Grand Rapids, MI: Revell, 1998, 2001), 123.
7. See *ESV Study Bible*, ed. Wayne Grudem (Wheaton, IL: Crossway, 2008), note on 1 Kings 19:11–12.
8. Phil Ryken, *When Trouble Comes* (Wheaton, IL: Crossway, 2016), 57.
9. Nancy Guthrie, *What Grieving People Wish You Knew about What Really Helps (and What Really Hurts)* (Wheaton, IL: Crossway, 2016), 23.
10. Susan Verstraete, "Isaac Watts—Rejected Suitor" (2006), accessed August 1, 2016, http://www.bulletininserts.org/bulletininsert.aspx ?bulletininsert_id=30.
11. See *ESV Study Bible*, note on 1 Cor. 10:19–20.
12. James Montgomery Boice, *The Gospel of John: The Coming of the Light*, vol. 1 (1999; repr., Grand Rapids, MI: Baker, 2005), 279.
13. Philip G. Ryken, *Jeremiah and Lamentations: From Sorrow to Hope*, Preaching the Word, ed. R. Kent Hughes (Wheaton, IL: Crossway, 2016), 270.

14. Barry Danylak, *Redeeming Singleness: How the Storyline of Scripture Affirms the Single Life* (Wheaton, IL: Crossway, 2010), 213–14.
15. Jen Hatmaker, Facebook post, April 23, 2016, https://www.facebook .com/permalink.php?story_fbid=946752262090436&id=203920953 040241.
16. Chelsen Vicari, "Jen Hatmaker, Blurry Lines, and Transformative Truth," *Faith and Chelsen* (blog), April 26, 2016, http://www .patheos.com/blogs/faithchelsen/2016/04/jen-hatmaker-blurry-lines -and-transformative-truth/.

General Index

Scripture Index

Convenient Devotionals
for Women on the Go
by Lydia Brownback

"Skillful devotionals for those who face the challenge to 'fit it all in.' Biblically rigorous and deeply perceptive. Godly insights from a godly sister."

ELYSE FITZPATRICK, author, *Because He Loves Me*

For more information, visit crossway.org.

Also Available from Lydia Brownback

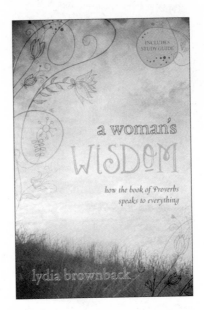

Unpacking the book of Proverbs, Lydia Brownback teaches women that all true wisdom springs from the fear of the Lord.

"Read and experience how God's wisdom is eloquent and transcendent while being concrete and practical at the same time."

PAUL DAVID TRIPP, President, Paul Tripp Ministries; author, *New Morning Mercies*

"In *A Woman's Wisdom*, we're invited to saturate ourselves in the source of true wisdom—the Scriptures—where we find what we need for living in a world full of distractions, decisions, dilemmas, disappointments, and delights."

NANCY GUTHRIE, Bible Teacher; author, Seeing Jesus in the Old Testament Bible study series

For more information, visit crossway.org.